Press

MEDALS AND INSIGNIA OF THE REPUBLIC OF VIETNAM AND HER ALLIES 1950-1975

By:
Colonel Frank Foster
with contributions from
Mr. John Sylester Jr.
and Mr. Ngan Dinh, ARVN

Library of Congress Control Number: 2019955422
Hardcover Edition ISBN - 978-1-884452-49-9
Softcover Edition ISBN - 978-1-884452-48-2

Copyright 2020 by MOA Press

All rights reserved. No part of this publication may be reproduced, stored in retrieval systems or transmitted by any means, electronic, mechanical or by photocopying, recording or by any information storage and retrieval system without permission from the publishers, except for the inclusion of brief quotations in a review.

Published by:

MOA Press (Medals of America Press)
114 Southchase Blvd. • Fountain Inn, SC 29644
Telephone: (800) 308-0849
www.moapress.com • www.usmedals.com

About the Author

COLONEL FRANK FOSTER

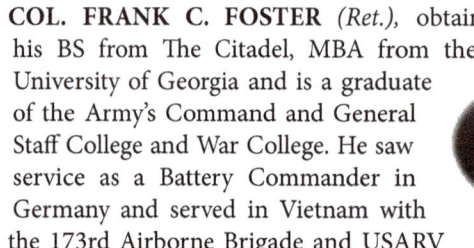

COL. FRANK C. FOSTER *(Ret.)*, obtained his BS from The Citadel, MBA from the University of Georgia and is a graduate of the Army's Command and General Staff College and War College. He saw service as a Battery Commander in Germany and served in Vietnam with the 173rd Airborne Brigade and USARV General Staff. In the Adjutant General's Corps, he served as the Adjutant General of the Central Army Group, the 4th Infantry Division and was the Commandant and Chief of the Army's Adjutant General's Corps from 1986 to 1990. His military service provided him a unique understanding of the Armed Forces Awards System. He currently operates Medals of America Press and is the author of the *Military Medals of America*, several books on the Air Force, Marines and Navy awards and coauthor of *The Decorations and Medals of the Republic of Vietnam*. He and his wife Linda, who was decorated with the Army Commander's Medal in 1990 for service to the Army, live in Greenville, South Carolina.

Grateful Acknowledgements

The author wish to express his deepest appreciation to the following individuals for their invaluable contributions. Without their unselfish efforts, this book would have ended as an unfilled dream.

Mr. John Sylvester Junior is responsible for researching and originally writing almost the entire text of this volume. Which was originally published in a book we did together titled: *The Decorations and Medals of the Republic of Vietnam and Her Allies, 1950 through 1975*. When I proposed a new and expanded edition John declined explaining that he was actually very busy improving his golf game during retirement. John lived in the far east as a child before World War II. After graduation from Williams College in 1952, he was in the Army Infantry with the Fifth Regimental Combat Team in the last stages of the Korean War. He was a Foreign Service Officer from 1955 to 1980, working primarily on Japan and Vietnam.

He served in the pacification program 1968 to 1970 in Chau Doc, Kien Giang and Binh Long provinces, and in the embassy in Saigon 1970 to 1972. During that period he acquired a real interest in the medals of Indochina and has written monographs and articles on Vietnamese awards as well as other awards of the different countries comprising Indochina. He later worked at North Carolina State University in Raleigh until recently when he is retired and devoted himself to polishing his golf game.

Special thanks to Mr. Ngan Dinh , formerly of the ARVN Airborne Division for his help with Vietnamese translations.

Colonel Gary L. Gresch for the cover photograph of his platoon in Vietnam.

Press
Table of Contents

Grateful Acknowledgements............................... 2
Short History of the Republic of Vietnam
and map.. 4
Introduction.. 6
Symbolism of the Medals 8
State, Republic and Loss of the South 10
The Medals 12
Procedures for Awards 14
Procedures for Wearing Military Medals 16
RVN National Order 18
RVN Military Awards Color Plates.............. 19-24
RVN Military Medal Descriptions 25-43
RVN Civilian Awards Color Plates.............. 44-52
Allied Awards Color Plates 53-55
RVN Civilian Medal Descriptions................. 56-58
RVN Unit Awards 69
Medals of the Allies 70
T'ai Federation
and Nung Autonomous Zone...................... 70-72
Empire of Annam 72-73
Republic of France 74-76
United States 77-80
Commonwealth 81-82
Republic of Korea 83
Kingdom of Thailand....................................... 84
Republic of the Philippines 85
Republic of China 86
International Commissions 87-88
Federal Republic of Germany
and the Knights of Malta................................. 89
RVN Memo on award of New Medals 90-91
RVN Army Uniforms and Insignia............... 92-93
RVN Navy Uniforms and Insignia.................... 94
RVN Air Force Uniforms and Insignia............. 95
RVN Shoulder Sleeve Insignia Examples 96-97
RVN Medal Certificates................................... 98
RVN Skill Badge Examples 99
RVN, USA and French Medals Examples........ 100
RVN, USA and French
Miniature Medals Examples.......................... 101
Commemorative Medals 102
Bibliography.. 103

This book is dedicated to the Vietnamese, American and Allies who earned the awards for valor and service during the long, tragic war in Vietnam. It is also dedicated to the families and friends who supported them.

CHRONOLOGICAL HISTORY OF THE STATE AND REPUBLIC OF VIETNAM

1949 Mar.		Vietnam made an Associated State of the French Union
1954 May		Dien Bien Phu falls
1954 July		Geneva Agreements bring cease fire, divide Vietnam
1954-55		Exodus of refugees from north
1955 Oct.		Republic of Vietnam proclaimed
1959		North Vietnam recommences effort to take the south
1960 Dec.		Hanoi forms National Liberation Front
1963 Nov.		Military coup kills Diem, First Republic ends
1964		Second Republic under Military Revolutionary Council
1967 Sept.		General Nguyen Van Thieu elected President
1968 Jan.		Communists attack at Tet
1970 Apr.		ARVN and U.S. forces enter Cambodia
1971 Feb.		ARVN makes incursion into Laos
1972		ARVN stops major communist offensive
1973 Jan.		Paris "Peace Agreement" signed
1973-74		ARVN and PAVN jostle for territory
1975 Jan.		PAVN captures Phuoc Long, with no U.S. reaction
1975 Mar.		Major PAVN offensive begins at Banmethuot
1975 Mar.		ARVN withdrawal from central Vietnam leads to panic
1975 Apr.		Final ARVN defense at Xuan Loc
1975 Apr.		Saigon is captured, and Republic falls

Two Vietnamese Army Berets with insignia. The dark beret on the bottom has a Ranger Beret badge which is a gold with a silver winged arrow and a yellow shield with three vertical red stripes. The top red beret has a gold bullion embroidered parachute insignia with the maker's trademark visible inside. A set of Vietnamese army parachute wings are shown in both metal and embroidery as well as an active jump status insignia. Vietnamese coins and paper money rest in the former paratrooper's Beret.

Introduction

During its short and tragic history, the Republic of Vietnam faced the usual problems of a newly independent nation compounded by armed communist assault. Its armed forces were in combat during most of the republics life, at times with valor and success, but in the end not with victory.

The United States, aided by others came to the defense of the Republic of Vietnam in an intervention that in the in failed. American forces lost no battles, but the cost grew too high in blood, money and politics.

Vietnamese, American, and allied Armed Forces personnel and many civilians received medals for their service in the war. Orders, decorations, and medals are symbols of courage and merit, as well as human vanity. They are, also perhaps, enduring fragments and mementos of history.

This book is intended to illustrate and describe all of the awards of the Republic of Vietnam. It also includes those of its allies for the war, along with the pertinent French and local ones. Included are short histories relevant to each one of these medals and other information that puts them in context. There are some additional sections that show examples of the uniforms, badges and shoulder sleeve insignia.

The color plates and written descriptions of the Vietnamese awards are in the order of precedence. The Republic of Vietnam had separate precedence for the military and civilian medals, but a set of military ribbon bars would have the military awards first and the civil medals following. Examples of the ribbon are shown on the page 17 and 45.

For each medal, an English and Vietnamese or other original name are given, followed by its number of classes and the date of establishment for the award. The purpose of the award is officially described as is best understood is also provided. Then follows a description of the planchet, which is a small medal disk which may or may not have raised edges, and of the ribbon with a listing of the various classes of the award. The ribbon colors are given in millimeters width except for the American ones which are in inches. Background comments are added with an indication of the difference between the Vietnamese and the American-made version. All pictures are of the original medals.

The relative rarity, and thus a rough guide as the cost of these medals is indicated by the scale of R (rarity) 1 to 10. R1 is the most common award seen on the military

Vietnamese National Order above with American made verison on the left.

Vietnamese manufactured Armed Forces Honor Medal First class with an American made verison.

market, and R 10 the rarest and most costly. These rarity scales are for the original made awards, not for American or recent made copies. Rarity can be affected at any time by the release to the market of an accumulation of these awards by a manufacturer or collector.

The rarity of the Vietnamese medals on the collectors market does not correspond to their value as an award when actually presented in Vietnam. The most common of the Vietnamese medals now seen for sale are the campaign medal, the Second Republic Military Medal, the Gallantry Cross, the Fifth Class of the National Order, the Armed Forces Honor Medals and the Staff Service Medals. The other military medals are sporadically for sale by the dealers. The civil medals are not currently often sold. The American-made versions of many Vietnamese medals are still available from dealers. Generally, all Vietnamese made medals have become scarcer on the market.

There are medals of the Republic of Vietnam currently being brought out of Saigon, although often in very poor condition. Somewhat like they have been buried, and others have been soiled or have incorrect ribbons. The price of these medals on the military or market is such now that it is quite possible enterprising merchants in Vietnam or elsewhere will start manufacturing the medals again. This is been done with some of the patches, which are often close in appearance to the original Vietnamese made shoulder sleeve insignia.

Armed Forces day in Saigon was the occasion for a formal parade and wear of the white uniform with decorations.

Compared to the drastic effect of condition on the price of coins, minor wear to medals does not usually hurt their value on the military market. Real damage to the medals and soiling of a suspension ribbon, however, adversely affect the value. A group of medals made up for wear adds additional value, but the authenticity of the group needs to be verified by questions and inspection.

Original Vietnamese award certificates are not common, and when paired with the award, the value is significantly increased. The higher orders sometimes came in special presentation boxes which should add to the value. The lower award usually came in a flimsy card board box, sometimes with interesting manufacturers printed labels on them.

Since it is now over 50 years since the fall of Saigon, you can expect to find fewer original South Vietnamese made awards available. The knowledge and information on the Republic's awards system is also disappearing. We hope this book will preserve the memory of the Republic and of its awards to the men and women who fought so hard for its preservation.

Vietnamese manufactured miniature medals mounted for wear compared to American made verisons.

ANATOMY AND SYMBOLISM OF THE DECORATIONS AND MEDALS

Orders, decorations, and medals can all be roughly described as awards, although they are different in character. Orders originated as symbols of membership in religious/military societies, or brotherhoods, such as the Order of the Knights of Malta. Today the highest awards of some countries are termed orders, and signify selection into an elite group of great distinction. They are normally given to people of high civil or military rank. Decorations, traditionally in the shape of crosses or stars, are awards given to an individual for valor or merit. Medals are generally given for service in a military campaign, for good conduct, or for other purposes, and usually signify a lesser level of distinction than a decoration. Medals, usually round in shape, can be either for wear or not, the latter often called table medals or medallions.

Napoleon, when he founded the French Legion of Honor in five classes, set the pattern for orders around the world, including the Republic of Vietnam National Order. The Grand Cross or First Class is worn across the shoulder with a wide ribbon of about 100mm. In addition, a star, called in French a plaque, is worn on the right or left breast. The Grand Officer or Second Class is usually just the star alone. The Commander or Third Class is worn from a ribbon around the neck called a cravat, sometimes in a wider width of about 50mm. The Officer or Fourth Class is worn from a ribbon with a large rosette (kind of a circular tuft of ribbon). The Knight or Fifth Class has a suspension ribbon without a rosette. Most French and Vietnamese ribbons are about 35mm in width.

Decorations will sometimes have separate awards or classes for officers and for enlisted personnel. The South Vietnamese usually distinguished awards for officers as first class and for enlisted personnel as second class. Enlisted personnel could qualify for first class under certain conditions.

Medals are a term sometimes applied to the entire field of decorations, but should only be applied to any award hanging from a ribbon. They may be gold, silver, bronze metal, etc., sometimes enamelled or gilded. The service medals are usually circular although the Vietnamese used many shapes, taking some patterns from French medals.

Orders, decorations and medals may or may not have a design or inscription on the back (reverse). Some South Vietnamese medals have a plain back. Those that do have, may have a simple inscription, often written around the word *VIỆT-NAM*.

South Vietnamese medals are mounted for wear in the same style as the French. The medal ribbon has a "u" shaped device with sharp pins for sticking into the uniform. American-made South Vietnamese medals come with a brooch on the ribbon for wearing purposes.

The ribbons, used to suspend the awards for wear, were designed in different colors that quickly identified the award. As it became too cumbersome to wear the medals on the uniform, the custom began in the 19th century to wear small pieces of the distinctive ribbons on the uniform as service bars. Examples of each RVN medal ribbon bar are shown on the back cover.

The ribbon can be made of fine silk, with or without a cloud-like moire pattern, or crude cotton weave, as are most Vietnamese ribbons. Occasionally stars or other symbols are woven in, or the stripes may be diagonal (as on several of the Vietnamese medals.) Sometimes the number or pattern of stripes may be used to indicate the respective classes of the award. Most Vietnamese service ribbons were sized 36mm by 10mm.

The red and yellow of the ribbon of the Vietnamese Cross of Gallantry are traditional auspicious colors of Vietnam and China, the same colors as the flag of the Republic of Vietnam. The design of the ribbon also resembles that of the French Croix de Guerre for overseas operations, on which the Cross of Gallantry was modeled. The green and yellow stripes of the French Indochina Medal are the same colors, but reversed, of the ribbon for the Tonkin Medal (given in the last century to the French army and navy as they originally conquered Vietnam).

The design of an order, decoration, or medal and the ribbon reflects symbolism by the form and ornamentation. Swords, anchors, or propellers on the planchet or in the angles of the cross may indicate awards respectively for the army, navy, and air force. A caduceus and a red cross indicate medical awards, and in Vietnam, as well as other parts of sinitic Asia, a dragon, scholar's scrolls, and bats all have auspicious meanings. Laurel leaves are symbols of honor from the Greeks and Romans. Palm wreaths are symbols of courage and strength.

On the suspension ribbon and the service bar, there may be devices or rosettes to indicate the class of the award. Devices may indicate the number of times it has been awarded, or just be a part of the design of the whole medal. For instance, on the ribbon of the Vietnamese Cross of Gallantry, following the practice of the French Croix de Guerre, there may be a bronze palm leaf, or a gold, silver, or bronze star indicating each award and the level of command at which the medal was bestowed.

The medal may have a special suspension piece tying it to the ribbon above. In the case of the Vietnamese Cross of Gallantry, this is a small design of dragons and clouds, both auspicious symbols in the Far East. The French Indochina Medal is suspended also by a dragon, indicating in this case, that the medal pertains to war in Vietnam.

The front or obverse of the planchet of the award is the main visible design, usually with special symbolism. The Vietnamese Cross of Gallantry resembles the French Croix de Guerre with the basic cross, but with dragons, swords, a map of Vietnam, and an appropriate motto added to distinguish it. The French Indochina Medal has the name of the Republic of France, the inscription *INDOCHINE*, a three-headed elephant called the Erawan symbolizing Laos, and the seven-headed cobra called a Naga symbolizing Cambodia. The back or reverse of the planchet, the less visible side, may be plain, have its own design, or have a simple inscription as in the case of the French Indochina Medal with a wreath and *CORPS EXPEDITIONNAIRE D'EXTREME ORIENT* for the troops who received it. Miniatures are smaller scale versions of the full decorations and medals. There was a vogue in Europe about the turn of the century for wearing half-scale medals, in part, perhaps just to avoid the weight of all the awards on the uniform! But miniatures now are intended exclusively for wearing with evening dress, either on the left lapel or breast. The Vietnamese followed the French practice in wearing miniatures of 14mm size. Americans miniatures, and our miniature copies of Vietnamese ones, are larger.

SYMBOLISM OF DECORATIONS AND MEDALS

Ribbon of a Medal

The ribbon (or riband) of a medal is a woven silk ribbon with or without moire or of other material, and of different widths and colors. Occasionally stars or symbols are woven into the ribbon. The colors are usually symbolic and can be arranged in different patterns (such as the diagonal bands on the RVN Staff Service Medal.) The ribbon can have extra stripes or bands to indicate the class of the award. Additionally a rosette or devices of different metals can be used to denote the classes of the awards.

Palm Device

Symbolism and Devices
Dragons, swords, palms, anchors, even bats, are often used to link the riband and the medallion. The dragon here represents Vietnam.

Dragon and Clouds

Symbols on the Medal
In this case, the Naga, the seven-headed cobra, represents Cambodia; the three-headed elephant represents Laos.

Swords
Denote a military or combat award.

The Republic of Vietnam Gallantry Cross

Name of the Medal
Sometimes expressed on the face or back of the medal, or in many cases metaphorically displayed.

The French Indochina Medal

STATE AND REPUBLIC OF VIETNAM AND THE LOSS OF THE SOUTH

The State of Vietnam was born as France grew increasingly frustrated in the protracted war with the Viet Minh. Finally reconciled to passing a measure of autonomy to the Vietnamese, the Elysee Accords of March 8, 1949, made Vietnam an Associated State of the French Union, although retaining French control over foreign policy and military affairs. On June 14, Bao Dai and High Commissioner Pignon formalized the agreement through an exchange of letters. Few Vietnamese Nationalists were impressed with the extent of French concessions. Bao Dai, unable to find a prestigious person who would join him, was forced initially to take the prime ministership himself. The State of Vietnam had its own flag, but over its first five years had weak governments which were all too identified with the French. Internal unity was also undercut by the feudal baronies of the sects in the south, and of the Dai Viet areas and the Catholic bishoprics of Phat Diem and Bui Chu in the north (with their militia called the "Mobile Units for the Defense of Christendom").

The French Army hoped that the new Vietnamese National Army created in its own image would relieve the Expeditionary Forces of much of the static defense duties. By the military convention of December 30, the new army's 1st Division was to be stationed in the south, the 2nd and 3rd Divisions in the north, and the 4th, a mountain division, stationed in Central Vietnam. There were to be 54 infantry and 2 parachute battalions and 4 artillery groups. It was formed partly by conscription and partly by incorporation of the militias, including the troops of the sects. By November 1953, there were some 200,000 in the National Army, 50,000 "supplementifs" or contract soldiers, and 78,000 in the police and militia, as well as 100,000 Vietnamese in the French regular forces.

While many of these troops fought well, overall they were a disappointment. The American General O'Daniel noted that their officers were "perhaps abnormally inclined to vanity, pretentiousness, and personal rivalries." The famous half-Vietnamese Colonel Jean Leroy, who trained the Catholic militia of Ben Tre, was reported as commenting that "the Vietnamese army was concerned much more with tailoring of uniforms and unearned decorations than with the primary purpose of combatting the Communist enemy." One problem was that many of the upper class officers did not understand their peasant troops. Morale often was poor; for instance, one whole battalion mutinied during Operation Atlante near Tuy Hoa in April 1954.

By the time of the Geneva Conference the French government had essentially decided to abandon Vietnam, and thus on June 4, 1954, "perfected" the independence of Vietnam. The State of Vietnam at Geneva protested the partitioning of its people and territory and said it would not accept limits on "organizing its defense in the manner it believes the most in conformity with its national interest." Bao Dai on June 14 offered the prime ministership to the stubborn and self-confident exile, Ngo Dinh Diem. With US support, Diem organized the huge exodus of refugees from the north and reconstituted a government in the south. Surprisingly he was able to buy off or beat down the sect armies (Cao Dai, with some 15,000 troops; the Hoa Hao with 8,000; the Binh Xuyen bandits with 2,000). He also replaced General Nguyen Van Hinh, a French citizen, and displaced Emperor Bao Dai after a rigged referendum. The Republic of Vietnam was proclaimed on October 26, 1955.

Diem, the Catholic mandarin, was honest and patriotic, but also autocratic, conservative, and an ineffectual administrator. His Can-Lao Nhan-Vi (Labor Personalist) Party was built up by his brother Ngo Dinh Nhu to provide an organizational base and an instrument against Diem's enemies. Diem favored the Catholic minority and alienated thus the other elements of the varied Vietnamese society. His land reform program had only limited success and the succeeding attempts to improve rural security through the founding of large agrovilles and then Malayan-type strategic hamlets were subject to poor execution and communist harassment. The Vietnamese Army was steadily expanded, but Diem was suspicious of the generals and valued personal loyalty over competence. The Vietnamese Army suffered a humiliating and revealing setback in January 1963 in the battle of Ap Bac against a smaller communist force.

In May 1963, an incident at Hue brought the Buddhists there into conflict with the regime. The heavy-handed suppression by Nhu's Special Forces provoked widespread criticism of Diem both in Vietnam and abroad. The generals then decided to remove Diem. On November 1, 1953, in a smoothly run coup led officially by General Duong Van Minh, Diem and his brother were killed and the First Republic ended.

The Second Republic under the Military Revolutionary Council began inauspiciously with a series of changes of power among the generals, first with the mini-coup of General Nguyen Khanh on January 29, 1964. This was followed by a continued slide of security in the countryside and by renewed Buddhist struggle. On February 20, 1965 the generals decided to oust Khanh. The following civil regime of Dr. Phan Huy Quat was later replaced by one led by Air Force General Nguyen Cao Ky. He, in turn, took second place under General Nguyen Van Thieu in the presidential election in September 1967.

By 1973, the ARVN had grown to 450,000 in 11 infantry, one Marine, and one Airborne division, plus some 25 Ranger battalions, one Special Forces group, 35 artillery battalions, and 6 independent armored cavalry regiments. The Navy had 40,275 personnel and the Air Force 50,000. Some 285,000 Regional Forces were in 1,700 rifle companies and 250,000 Popular Forces in 7,500 village defense platoons. Of the divisions, the highly regarded 1st, the newly formed 3rd, and the 2nd were in I Corps in Central Vietnam; the 22nd was in the highlands and the 23rd on the coast of II Corps; the 5th, 18th, and 25th in III Corps; the 7th, 9th, and 21st in the Delta in IV Corps; and the excellent Airborne Division and Marine Division in strategic reserve. The elite units were noticeable for their berets; green for Marines, red for paratroops, black for armored troops, and maroon for Rangers.

With the infusion of American arms, advice, and training, the ARVN and RF/PF steadily improved. The enthusiastic American units, however, tended to push the ARVN aside to get into battle, a situation the ARVN, knowing it was a long war, was pleased to accept. By 1969, when the US decided to back out of the war, the ARVN had not built the requisite experience and confidence. The ARVN officer corps and commanders varied too widely in quality. Nevertheless many of the ARVN units, ranging from the Airborne to individual RF companies, were excellent.

While the ARVN remained steadily engaged through the Tet battles and afterwards, the first major campaign on its own took place in Cambodia in 1970 under the flamboyant and capable General Do Cao Tri, who was later killed in a helicopter crash.

The 1971 ARVN incursion into Laos, called Lam Son 719, ended with the ARVN units congregated in that inhospitable terrain by the Ho Chi Minh road network. In the spring of 1972, the North Vietnamese undertook a major offensive. In central Vietnam, the PAVN (Communist People's Party of Vietnam) broke the ARVN 3rd Division and seized most of Quang Tri province, but were stopped by the able General Ngo Quang Truoung after hard fighting. At An Loc, just north of Saigon, ARVN and RF units, with the help of B-52's used tactically, withstood a bitter siege. But with the departure of the allies, the number of combat divisions on the side of the South had fallen from 22 to 13.

After the 1973 "Peace Agreement" the ARVN and PAVN jostled for territory. In January 1975, the North Vietnamese seized Phuoc Long province. When this did not bring a US reaction, the PAVN went ahead with plans for a major offensive. After grinding and inconclusive combat north of Hue in early 1975, the PAVN attacked Banmethuot in the highlands in March. President Thieu decided to abandon the highlands and also withdraw the Airborne Division from central Vietnam for use in reserve. While perhaps strategically sound, these moves provoked panic, and South Vietnam crumbled. Individuals units fought well, notably the RF in Binh Dinh and the Airborne and 18th Division at Xuan Loc, but the momentum of the PAVN carried them to Saigon. Thieu resigned and the Americans flew out. A last minute peace government of General Duong Van Minh was contemptuously swept up by the victors and the Republic of Vietnam died.

Poster of Recruitment for ARVN Airborne Battalion

THE MEDALS

As a display of its new partial sovereignty, the State of Vietnam in 1950 issued medals of its own to go along with the new flag and National Army. Recommendations for awards were to be sent on January 1 of each year to the Imperial Chancellery for the final decisions of His Majesty the Chief of State. Of the early medals, only the Wound Medal was inscribed "State of Vietnam", later it was changed to "Republic of Vietnam".

After 1954, Vietnam was effectively split with the communist in the north and a pro-western government in the south. The Republic of Vietnam developed an extensive awards system patterned mainly on the French model. Only the civilian *Kim Khánh* decoration retained true native flavor. A review of French medals and devices reveal the originals of some of the South Vietnamese medals.

The *Kim Khánh* was a direct link with pre-French Annamite decorations: the Khanh, Boi, Tien and Bai. The highest decoration for the Emperor, made of jade, was the Ngoc-Khanh. The *Kim-Khánh*, kim meaning made of gold, was divided into classes. The Boi, was for women, and the Tien was a lesser distinction. These decorations were quite different from western decorations. They were normally beautifully engraved or cast plaques of precious metal suspended by a woven red neck cord.

The French-influenced medals, such as the Vietnamese Military Medal, also altered designs with the political changes. This, of course, was also in keeping with French tradition, as noted in the many redesigns of the French Legion of Honor. The Military Medal, for example, changed from a visage of the Emperor Bao Dai to a grove of bamboo, which was dropped as too associated with President Diem and replaced with a motto more becoming to the Second Republic.

The earlier medals were originally manufactured in France and reflected French quality. Some of the Vietnamese-made medals are of similar fine quality, but most are of lesser quality and some quite shoddy. Medals sometimes were manufactured without the correct, or any, marking on the reverse. Among the civil medals particularly, there are a number of manufacturer's variations. Some Vietnamese medals were also said to have been procured from manufacturers in Taiwan.

Most of the Vietnamese military awards and a few of the civil ones were manufactured also in the US or abroad reportedly by Wolf Brown and Vanguard, probably for US servicemen who wanted their Vietnamese awards to be of a quality that would match their American awards. These US-made medals generally are of neater and brighter metal and enamel work. They usually (but not always) have American-style ribbon with bound edges, shorter suspension, and a catch-pin fastener. They sometimes appear quite different from the Vietnamese-made ones, the American-made National Order, for instance, being quite flattened.

Some Vietnamese (and American) medals were also manufactured in Japan for sale for wear by US sailors and marines in dress ceremonies. The Vietnamese Campaign Medal has been extensively manufactured abroad since it was earned by almost all foreign troops who fought with the Republic of Vietnam. Those won by Australian and New Zealand servicemen are engraved on the back with the name and unit designation in standard Commonwealth style.

During the Diemist period the Gallantry Cross was only sparingly bestowed. Later the standards for its award decreased and combat increased. Experienced infantry soldiers might have received well over a dozen of the Gallantry Crosses, and thus have to wear the medals with a long ribbon covered with the devices for the multiple awards.

As the war progressed, there was still the occasional formal parade such as the major one in Saigon on Armed Forces Day, June 17, 1971. The chief of staff, General Cao Văn Viên, was pictured in white formal uniform with his left breast covered with four rows of medals. The flag bearer in parades was customarily an old soldier who would wear medals extending back often to the French period. The Republic developed an increasingly extensive system of military and civil awards, and life in the units and garrisons, as well as in the offices of the respective civil ministries and services, was often marked with presentation ceremonies. Although many were given for reasons of rank or length of service, the war provided all too many valid occasions for the presentation of awards for bravery and wounds.

Ribbon bars were usually sewn on black felt, sometimes covered with plastic or made up in a semi-rolled fashion. The ribbon bars were often worn in field dress. Many ARVN officers had served in civil capacities, such as district or province chiefs, and their sets often contained ribbons of the civil awards.

The flag of the State and of the Republic of Vietnam was gold — the Imperial color — with three horizontal red stripes representing the three traditional regions of the country. This handsome flag was seen everywhere in the Republic, partly because of its auspicious colors and partly because of the government's intensive efforts to promote it as a patriotic symbol. The symbol of the State was the Imperial dragon, a very traditional symbol. The First Republic used a grove of bamboo. The arms of the Second Republic were a shield with the design of the flag, but with the stripes vertical, supported by two dragons.

Civil awards came with buttonhole ribbons, single miniature strips or small bows often with the devices or, in the cases of first class medals with rosettes, with a small rosette for the coat lapel.

Fourrageres were in the colors of red (predominating) and yellow for units that had received the National Order, green and yellow for the Military Medal, and yellow and red for the Cross of Gallantry. Units that had received unit honors nine times had a fourragere in red with lesser markings in yellow and green. There was also a fourragere in white for Popular Forces units cited at the armed forces level. These awards and the Civil Actions Medal were also exhibited as unit citation streamers inscribed with the name and date of the action and affixed to the unit flag. Unit awards of the military and police were also worn following American practice as ribbons in gold frames on the uniform. Awards of the fourrageres to American military units or personnel was not authorized.

Major General Nguyen Vinh Nghi
April 30, 1971

PROCEDURES FOR AWARDS

Following the traditions of the Annamese mandarinate and the French bureaucracy, the Republic of Vietnam had extensive regulations on the procedures for awards. Probably in practice, it was not much different from how it was done in most countries.

Recommendations for awards for valor and merit needed to be well justified and had to go through the proper channels with an array of approving signatures. The awards were, of course, scaled by rank, with the highest ones appropriate only for senior officers and officials. Military awards would be processed by the ARVN's Adjutant General Division. Most awards had to be approved at the Saigon level of the ARVN or the civil ministries. The Cross of Gallantry could be awarded on the spot at the discretion of the commander or province chief, but, even then, needed to be justified on paper.

Careful regulations also detailed the required length of service or other conditions that allowed their bestowal on Americans and other allies (e.g., Joint General Staff Memorandum 910/TTM/VP/PCP/3). For senior officers the usual awards were the National Order and the Army, Air Force, and Navy Distinguished Service Orders; many American generals and admirals came back from duty in Vietnam with these exotic-looking medals and ribbons to decorate their uniforms. The customary awards for American and other advisors of lesser rank were the Armed Forces Honor Medal (French army advisors before 1955 often receiving this), the Staff Service Medal, the Technical Service Medal, and the Training Service Medal. For valor the usual award was the Gallantry Cross. And for work in a specialized field, such as an advisor to the *Chieu Hoi* program encouraging Viet Cong to rally to the government, it might be the proper civil award, in this case one of the two classes of the Psychological Warfare Medal. In practice most medals of the Republic were open to presentation to American and allied personnel.

Medals were usually bestowed in a military or civil ceremony. The original decree of His Majesty Bao Dai establishing the National Order specified, for instance, that it was to be presented by the Chief of State or his designee with honors paid by at least one company of troops. The decree also specified the size of the honor guard for the awardee's funeral! Following French practice, Vietnamese medals were affixed with a two pronged pin. This allowed the award to be stuck on the jacket without fumbling, but with some fear on the awardee's part that the pin could go though the shirt into the skin.

An American officer or enlisted man receiving a Vietnamese award then, of course, had to comply with our military regulations to accept and wear the award. Governments generally are leery about their military and civilian accepting foreign titles and medals, believing, and not without reason, that judgement may be compromised by what is a flattering little honor or, in effect, a bribe. MACV (Military Assistance Command, Vietnam) thus set careful limits on what medals could be received. For instance, Special Forces personnel, amply decorated by Vietnamese colleagues in the highlands, were only allowed officially to keep some of them, mainly standard awards received by many other Army servicemen. The Department of State required that all Vietnamese and foreign awards to American civil advisors be surrendered. In a few cases they were returned with official authorizations, but most were later disposed of.

Along with the medal, Vietnamese, American, and other allied recipients were supposed to receive a copy of the memorandum citing the regulations and detailing the circumstances justifying the bestowal. They also received an award document. These were often large and colorful, showing a picture of the award or other embellishments, and having the appropriate red seal and signatures. In many cases the Americans never actually received the documents, although the authorized bestowal may be indicated on the American service records. Apparently, to sell at a good profit, totally inauthentic blank award documents for the Cross of Gallantry and Vietnamese insignia are being now sold in the U.S.

Following American practice, the Republic gave unit awards to particular ARVN, American, and allied units that distinguished themselves in the war. Actually the first such unit award was the State of Vietnam Ribbon of Friendship given in 1954 primarily to the US Navy for help in evacuating refugees from the north to the south. During the course of our major involvement in the war the unit awards were the Gallantry Cross and the Civil Actions Medal. The late authorized Military Merit Medal unit award, and the Police Honor and Merit Medal unit awards, apparently were never received by Americans.

Our servicemen who served in the honored units were authorized to wear the Vietnamese Unit Awards. They are worn in the standard gold frame on the right breast for American Army personnel, and with a smaller frame among the other ribbons on the left breast for US Air Force, Navy, and Marine personnel. ARVN personnel wore a fourragere after five or more presentations of the Gallantry Cross to their unit, but wear of ARVN fourrageres was not authorized for American service personnel, although French and Belgian fourrageres had been authorized for our earlier wars. These awards were also displayed as streamers on both the ARVN and other services, division, regiment and other lesser unit colors.

U.S. made verison

PROCEDURE FOR WEARING REPUBLIC OF VIETNAM MEDALS FOR RVNAF PERSONNEL

According to Decree No. 244/CL/LDQG/SL — 13 June, 1967

Order of Wearing:
RVNAF medals are worn in the following order from the center to the left side of the breast.

National Order of Vietnam	Bảo-Quốc Huân-Chương
Military Merit Medal	Quân-Công Bội-Tinh
Army Distinguished Service Order	Lục-Quân Huân-Chương
Air Force Distinguished Service Order	Không-Lực Huân-Chương
Navy Distinguished Service Order	Hải-Quân Huân-Chương
Army Meritorious Service Medal	Lục-Quân Vinh-Công Bội-Tinh
Air Force Meritorious Service Medal	Không-Quân Vinh-Công Bội-Tinh
Navy Meritorious Service Medal	Hải-Quân Vinh-Công Bội-Tinh
Special Service Medal	Biệt-Công Bội-Tinh
Gallantry Cross	Anh-Dũng Bội-Tinh
Air Gallantry Cross	Phi-Dũng Bội-Tinh
Navy Gallantry Cross	Hải-Dũng Bội-Tinh
Hazardous Service Medal	Ưu-Dũng Bội-Tinh
Life Saving Medal	Nhân-Dũng Bội-Tinh
Loyalty Medal	Trung-Chánh Bội-Tinh
Wound Medal	Chiến-Thương Bội-Tinh
Armed Forces Honor Medal	Danh-Dự Bội-Tinh
Leadership Medal	Chỉ-Đạo Bội-Tinh
Staff Service Medal	Tham-Mưu Bội-Tinh
Technical Service Medal	Kỹ-Thuật Bội-Tinh
Training Service Medal	Huấn-Vụ Bội-Tinh
Civil Actions Medal	Dân-Vụ Bội-Tinh
Good Conduct Medal	Quân-Phong Bội-Tinh
Campaign Medal	Chiến-Dịch Bội-Tinh
Military Service Medal	Quân-Vụ Bội-Tinh
Air Service Medal	Không-Vụ Bội-Tinh
Navy Service Medal	Hải-Vụ Bội-Tinh

** *See back cover for layout of ribbons in correct order.*

The Medal of Unity was awarded to civilians and the Medal of Sacrifice was intended for next of kin of servicemen killed in action. Neither was worn thus by military personnel in uniform. It is not known what the precedence was for the Medal for Campaigns Outside of the Frontier (*Chiến-Trường Ngoại-Biên Bội-Tinh*) and for the Air Force Northern Expeditionary Medal (*Không-Quân Bắc-Tiến Bội-Tinh*).

ARVN regulations stated the following: when a medal has been awarded more than five times, the recipients may wear additional pendant medals or ribbons in order to have enough space for placing all the devices. These devices must be exhibited in accordance with the order of precedence and not the date of presentation.

Republic of Vietnam civilian medals will be worn according to the presentation date of the award except for those in which an official document has been published by the Republic of Vietnam government which prescribes the order of wearing.

When equivalent awards are presented by other armed services, recipients will wear the medal or ribbon of their service first followed by the medals or ribbons received from other services, according to the presentation date of the award.

Foreign medals: Foreign awards will be worn to the left of all RVN medals or ribbons according to the presentation date of the award without regard to the level of the medals.

Several medals received from the same country, however, may be worn side by side in accordance with the level of the medals awarded.

Special Circumstances:
(1) When recipients wear the *Formal Ceremony Uniform*, either pendant medals or service ribbons are worn depending on which has been prescribed.

A special regulation does apply, however, for the RVN's two highest awards as follows: *The National Order of Vietnam, First and Second Classes, will always be worn as pendant medals with the above uniform.*

The Military Ribbons of the Republic of Vietnam

(2) When recipients wear the *Informal Ceremony Uniform*, medals at all levels, including the National Order, First and Second Classes, will be worn as service ribbons.

(3) Personnel who have been awarded the same type of medal many times will wear:

(a) *Only the highest class of this medal received and in the following order of precedence:*

-- National Order.
-- Army Distinguished Service Order.
-- Air Force Distinguished Service Order.
-- Navy Distinguished Service Order.
-- Good Conduct Medal.
-- Military Service Medal.
-- Air Service Medal.
-- Navy Service Medal.
-- Other types of medals.

(b) *Types of medals that may be awarded several times for meritorious service or achievement with each award represented by a device are as follows:*

-- Gallantry Cross.
-- Air Gallantry Cross.
-- Navy Gallantry Cross.
-- Wound Medal.
-- Armed Forces Honor Medal.
-- Civil Action Medal.
-- Campaign Medal.
-- Other types of medals.

Recipients will wear the above medals with all devices placed thereon. If there are many levels to be displayed, devices representing the levels will be arranged according to the levels, not the date of presentation.

17

1-2-3-4-5 NATIONAL ORDER
Bảo-Quốc Huân-Chương
five classes — Aug. 15, 1950

The National Order of the Republic of Vietnam was established in the summer of 1950 when the State of Vietnam became a part of the French Union. The award was patterned after Napoleon's Legion of Honor of 1812 and the French Colonial Order of the Dragon of Annam. The Dragon of Annam belonged to the independent monarch under French control.

French Legion of Honor   **Order of the Dragon of Annam**

In 1802 Napolean Bonaparte, then First Counsul, instituted the Legion d' Honneur as a reward for both military valor and civic accomplishment. At first the Order only had 4 classes; Grand Officier, Commandant, Officier and Chevalier. A fifth class was added in 1805 and became the top class known as the Grand Croix. The Vietnamese National Order reflected the French influence by having five classes with similar insignia and service ribbons with rosettes and silver and gold wings in the same manner as the French. The ribbon of the National Order is copied from the ribbon of the Order of the Dragon of Annam, and the green dragon is still present on the suspension of the medallion.

Purpose: The original 1950 decree issued in Cannes, France by the Emperor Bao Dai states:

"The National Order is designed to reward persons living or dead who have distinguished themselves by grandiose works, by remarkable deeds in the discharging of their duty or by their bravery and those who have honored and served the country by their lofty virtues or their outstanding knowledge. The National Order is also designed to reward the various organizations of the Army, the officially recognized groups, the administrative agencies (provinces, municipalities, towns, delegations, cantons, villages, districts) actuated by a lofty spirit of sacrifice and bravery and which have carried out actions whose glamour glorifies the country. Moreover, the National Order may be awarded to foreigners for diplomatic reasons.

The National Order may be awarded on a civil or military basis."

Description: The cross of the National Order is five patterned rays in gold, having at its center a red disk on which there is engraved with gold letters the inscription: *Tổ-Quốc Tri-ân* (the Gratitude of the Fatherland). The edge of the centered disk has a Greek key design border of gold on an azure blue background. This Greek border connects the five arms of the star (patterned rays). The distance between the lower arms of the star (rays), below the center disk is adorned with a coiled dragon's tail in green enamel. The suspension of the star consists of a dragon's head with a face of yellow gold with a green crest on either side. The ribbon is 34mm wide, yellow 6mm, red 22mm, yellow 6mm.

Grand Cross or First class - sash and star.

Description: The Grand Cross of the Order or National Order First Class is composed of both a star and the planchet hung from the 101mm sash ribbon worn across the shoulder. The sash ribbon is yellow 12mm, red 77mm and yellow 12mm. The sash badge is the same 65mm as the cravat badge of the third class. The star is the basic design except the rays (arms of the star), central disk, and surrounding border are all in gold. The spaces between the rays and a narrow strip around the central disk are composed of silver brilliants. The star is 95mm across and has no suspension ribbon but is mounted directly by use of prongs which pierce the clothing. The ribbon service bar has a rosette with gold wings.

Grand Officer or Second class - star.

Description: The star is as described above, 95mm across. The ribbon service bar has a rosette with one gold and one silver wing.

 **Commander or Third Class** - cravat.

Description: The cravat badge is as above, 65mm. It is worn around the neck. The ribbon service bar has a rosette with silver wings. The ribbon was originally specified to be 40mm, but in practice was 35mm.

 **Officer or Fourth Class** - ribbon with rosette.

Description: The same breast badge (cross) as the Third Class, but smaller, 43mm. The ribbon service bar has a rosette.

 **Knight or Fifth Class**.

Description: Same as above, 43mm. The ribbon service bar is without rosette.

National Order of Vietnam

Plate 1

2. National Order Star for First Class and Second Class
pgs. 18 & 25

1. National Order Sash and Badge First Class
pgs. 18 & 25

Plate 2

4. National Order, Officer or Fourth Class **pgs. 18 & 25**

3. National Order, Commander or Third Class **pgs. 18 & 25**

5. National Order, Knight or Fifth Class **pgs. 18 & 25**

6. Military Merit Medal State of Vietnam **pg. 27**

7. Military Merit Medal First Republic **pg. 27**

8. Military Merit Medal Second Republic **pg. 27**

Plate 3

9. Army Distinguished Service Order **pg. 28**

10. Air Force Distinguished Service Order **pg. 28**

11. Navy Distinguished Service Order **pg. 29**

12. Army Meritorious Service Medal **pg. 29**

13. Air Force Meritorious Service Medal **pg. 30**

14. Navy Meritorious Service Medal **pg. 30**

15. Special Service Medal **pg. 30**

16. Gallantry Cross **pg. 31**

Plate 4

17. Air Gallantry Cross *pg. 32*

18. Navy Gallantry Cross *pg. 32*

19. Hazardous Service Medal *pg. 33*

20. Life Saving Medal *pg. 33*

21. Loyalty Medal *pg. 33*

22. Wound Medal *pg. 34*

23. Armed Forces Honor Medal First Class *pg. 34-35*

24. Armed Forces Honor Medal Second Class *pg. 34-35*

Plate 5

25. Leadership Medal *pg. 36*
26. Staff Service Medal *pg. 37*
27. Technical Service Medal *pg. 37*
28. Training Service Medal *pg. 38*

29. Civil Actions Medal *pg. 38*
30. Good Conduct Medal *pg. 39*
31. Campaign Medal *pg. 39*
32. Military Service Medal *pg. 40*

Plate 6

33. Air Service Medal **pg. 40**

34. Navy Service Medal Version 1 **pg. 41**

35. Navy Service Medal Version 2 **pg. 41**

36. Navy Service Medal Version 3 **pg. 41**

37. Unity Medal **pg. 42**

38. Medal of Sacrifice **pg. 42**

39. Medal for Campaigns Outside the Frontier **pg. 44**

40. Air Force Northern Expeditionary Medal **pg. 45**

1-2-3-4-5 NATIONAL ORDE
Bảo-Quốc Huân-Chương

Background: The First Class or Grand Cross was intended for the most senior officers and officials of both Vietnam and allies and friendly countries. Lower classes of the order were intended for lower-ranked recipients, but a field grade officer would be the normal recipient of the knight's class. Senior American advisors often numbered this among their awards after duty there during the war. The star for the first class was worn on the right breast when the sash was also worn, and on the left breast when the sash was not worn. The Star for the Second Class was worn on the right breast (see page 86).

Some pictures of this order show a yellow ribbon with three red stripes, the design of the national flag, but this ribbon was apparently never used. Reportedly this ribbon was made in Paris before it was found that the State of Vietnam intended to use instead the ribbon design of the Order of The Dragon of Annam. The original decree of Bao Dai specified that "when the National Order is awarded on a military basis, the ribbon has, in addition, on each edge, borders of gold thread." This apparently was never put into effect.

The Vietnamese-made version of the National Order are relatively well made. The French-made versions are still better made, with finer enamel, and slightly heavier in appearance. A US-made version is curiously different, quite flat in contrast to the originals. The star of the order was made by Phuoc Thanh in Saigon in both an inferior quality and in a high silver content, one of those resembling the French pieces.

There is also an interesting rare version of the National Order, seen only in the Fifth Class, that was reportedly intended for veterans. It can be with the normal green enamel or without any color enameling, and has the inscription *QUỐC-GIA LAO-TƯỞNG*.

Rarity: First Class R-8; Second Class R-8; Third Class R-6; Fourth Class R-3; Fifth Class R-2

Special Version for Veterans

During the Vietnam War, the National Order of Vietnam was bestowed on several members of the United States military, most of whom were senior military and political advisors to the South Vietnamese government. The decoration could also be awarded posthumously.

Since the National Order of Vietnam was both a civil and a military decoration, it was displayed above all other awards when worn on a military uniform. A purely military equivalent of the decoration was the Vietnam Military Merit Medal, awarded only to members of the military.

6-7-8 MILITARY MERIT MEDAL
Quân-Công Bội-Tinh
August 15, 1950

Purpose: For the reward of aspirants (officer candidates), non-commissioned officers and enlisted men, chiefs of state and general officers, for feats of arms or distinction in bravery or devotion to duty, seniority, and professional conscientiousness, or specifically for citation at the Armed Forces level, or for wounds in combat, heroism, and for distinguished honorable service for 13 years.

Description: A round gold-colored medal, 35mm in diameter topped by a disk representing an arms trophy, with variations as follows: the ribbon is white 2mm, green 7mm, yellow center 16mm, with seven thread-like green stripes 1mm apart grouped in center, green 7mm, white 2mm.

(6) Award of the State of Vietnam
Description: Front: in the center the head of Emperor Bao Dai, surrounded with a thin ribbon inscribed *ĐỨC BẢO ĐẠI QUỐC TRƯỞNG* (His Majesty Bao Dai, chief of state), in turn surrounded by a wreath; Back: in the center the inscription *TỔ QUỐC TRÊN HẾT* (The Fatherland Over All), surrounded by a lined ribbon and a wreath. Suspension is by a single gold palm leaf crossed by swords and surrounded with a circle. This was manufactured in bronze reportedly by Arthus Bertrand, and also in gilt by Drago, with their name on the reverse of the suspension.

(7) Award of the First Republic
Description: Front: in the center a grove of bamboo, surrounded with a thin ribbon inscribed *QUÂN-CÔNG BỘI-TINH*, in turn surrounded by a wreath; Back: in the center a circle inscribed *VIỆT-NAM CỘNG HOA* with parallel lines above and below, surrounded with a thin ribbon as the front inscribed *QUÂN-CÔNG BỘI-TINH*, in turn surrounded by a wreath. Suspension is as above. There is a version manufactured by Drago which has the thin ribbon on the front, not inscribed and a back the same as number 6.

(8) Award of the Second Republic
Description: Front: in the center, instead of bamboos, the inscription *TỔ-QUỐC-TRI-ÂN* (The Gratitude of the Fatherland). Back and suspension as above.

Unit Award (*Huy-Hiệu Tuyên-Công Đơn-Vị*) Apparently authorized circa 1974.
Description: The ribbon is in a gold frame with a leaf pattern.

French Medaille Militaire

Background: This was equivalent of the French Medaille Militaire. It was awarded in only one class. It was a prestigious award for NCO's and general officers. The design changes reflect the political changes from Bao Dai, to Diem, to the post-coup government. Vietnamese-made versions of this award vary widely in quality and include heavy, solid pieces and light, hollow pieces. A US-made version closely resembles the Vietnamese-made, but the US-version has a smooth central disk behind the inscription, in contrast to the light pebbling of the Vietnamese-made ones. It could be awarded or posthumously presented to allied non-commissioned officers and enlisted men for valor, but few Americans, if any, received this medal. When first established it came with an annual allowance of 300 piastres.

Rarity: State of Vietnam R-5; First Republic R-8; Second Republic R-1

Military Merit Medal State of Vietnam

Military Merit Medal First Republic

Military Merit Medal Second Republic

Military Merit Medal Second Republic American

Military Merit Medal Second Republic American Miniature

Reverse

9. ARMY DISTINGUISHED SERVICE ORDER
Lục-Quân Huân-Chương
two classes - June 5, 1964

Purpose: For citations and wounds in combat or line of duty, or exceptional achievements that reflect great credit or benefit to the Army in any field.

Description: Front: a white Maltese-type cross except the rays are split down the center, with gold trident heads between the rays, and in the center, a red disk with three thin triangles in gold, and around an orange ribbon inscribed *LỤC-QUÂN HUÂN-CHƯƠNG* in gold, 35mm; Back: stamped *VIỆT-NAM* in a lined circle. The suspension ribbon is an odd embroidered design of two pieces that cross each other three times. The left top is brown and the right is green, ending up with a hanging thread fringe of the colors on the opposite side. The service bar is yellow with an embroidered design like an M on top of a W, with lines sloping right in green and rising to the right in brown.

First Class
Description: The ribbon is with a rosette on the suspension ribbon, and on the service bar.

Second Class
Description: The ribbon is without a rosette.

Background: This award with its odd-looking ribbon was for senior army officers, including America and other allies. The US version closely resembles the Vietnamese-made ones except that the enamel is neater and on the reverse the inscription *VIỆT-NAM* in a lined circle is smaller. The rosette is smaller and usually placed at the top instead of the middle of the suspension. The first-made Army DSO's, perhaps manufactured in France, were noticeably better made and larger in size, being 40mm in diameter. The three triangles in the central disk may represent the three regions of Vietnam. It was considered appropriate for foreign officers who should receive an award higher than the Gallantry Cross with palm, but did not merit the National Order.

Rarity: First Class R-5; Second Class R-4

*ARVN DSO
2d Class
American*

*ARVN DSO
First Class
Vietnamese*

10. AIR FORCE DISTINGUISHED SERVICE ORDER
Không-Lực Huân-Chương
two classes — June 4, 1964

Purpose: For citations and wounds in combat or line of duty, or exceptional achievements that reflect great credit or benefit to the Air Force in any field.

Description: Front: a gold four-pointed star with stylized jet planes in silver in each angle, space between in black, 50mm across (or smaller depending on manufacturer); Back: stamped *KHÔNG-LỰC HUÂN-CHƯƠNG* in a circle. Suspension is by a pair of gold wings. The ribbon is red 5mm, blue 27mm, red 5mm.

First Class
Description: There is a rosette on the suspension ribbon and service bar.

Second Class
Description: The ribbon is without a rosette.

Background: These Air Force DSO's come in large and small sizes, the stars being respectively 50mm or 35mm from horizontal tip to tip, but with no significance in the different sizes. The US-made version closely resembles Vietnamese-made ones (and has light blue paint behind the jet planes), but on the reverse is the inscription *VIỆT-NAM* in a neat-lined circle.

Rarity: First Class R-5; Second Class R-4

First Class

Second Class

*AFVN DSO
First Class
Vietnamese*

*First Class
Miniature
Ameican*

11 NAVY DISTINGUISHED SERVICE ORDER
Hải-Quân Huân-Chương
two classes — June 5, 1964

Purpose: For citations and wounds in combat or line of duty, or exceptional achievements that reflect great credit or benefit to the Navy in any field.

Description: Front: an eight-pointed silver star with a gold wreath underneath, and in the center a gold disk with crossed anchors and a traditional stylized grenade, and around a dark blue ribbon inscribed HẢI-QUÂN HUÂN-CHƯƠNG in gold, 45mm; Back: stamped VIỆT-NAM in a lined circle with HẢI-QUÂN HUÂN-CHƯƠNG around. The suspension ribbon is an odd embroidered design of two pieces that cross each other three times, the one on the left at the top being white, and on the right being blue, ending up with a hanging thread fringe of the colors on the opposite side. The service bar is yellow with an embroidered design like an M on top of a W, with the lines that slope down to the right in blue and those that rise to the right in white.

First Class
Description: There is a rosette on the suspension ribbon and on the service bar.
Second Class
Description: Ribbon is without a rosette.

Background: This was for senior Vietnamese and Allied naval officers and was received by a number of American admirals. The US-made version is entirely gold with a thinner wreath, indented central disk, and larger letters on the ribbon around the disk; the rosette is smaller and placed at the top instead of the middle of the suspension. A Japanese-made version is closely similar to the Vietnamese-made one, but more finely made. The star design is the traditional navy compass rose.

Rarity: First Class R-6; Second Class R-5

Navy DSO !st Class American   *Navy DSO 2d Class Vietnamese*

12. ARMY MERITORIOUS SERVICE MEDAL
Lục-Quân Vinh-Công Bội-Tinh
June 5, 1964

Purpose: For NCO's and enlisted men for citations and wounds in combat or line of duty, or exceptional achievements that reflect great credit or benefit to the Army in any field.

Description: Front: a gold Maltese cross with the center of the rays indented, with a red disk in the center with crossed rifles and sword, surrounded with a gold ribbon with inscription LỤC-QUÂN VINH-CÔNG BỘI-TINH and with a green wreath, 38mm; Back: stamped in a circle "VIETNAM" surrounded with inscription B.Q.P. VA C.C.B. above, and T.T.S.N. - C.C.B. below — another version with just VIỆT-NAM in a large-lined circle. The ribbon is brown 10mm, green 3mm, red 12mm, green 3mm, brown 10mm.

Background: Originally produced Army Meritorious Service Medals were appreciably larger in size, 45mm in diameter. The American manufactured version of this medal has an incorrect ribbon that is red with two light blue stripes. The US-made badge has a wreath with real enamel and on the reverse the inscription VIỆT-NAM in a lined circle. It was authorized to be awarded to allied enlisted personnel.

Rarity: R-3

Ameican shown with the wrong ribbon   *Vietnamese*

13 AIR FORCE MERITORIOUS SERVICE MEDAL
Không-Quân Vinh-Công Bội-Tinh — **June 5, 1964**

Purpose: For NCO's and enlisted men of the Air Force for citations and wounds in combat or line of duty, or exceptional achievements that reflect great credit on or benefit to the Air Force in any field.

Description: Front: silver four-pointed star with stylized jet planes in gold in each angle with the space between in black, 40mm across (depending on manufacturer); Back: stamped *KHÔNG-QUÂN VINH-CÔNG BỘI-TINH VIỆT-NAM* in circle with small four-pointed star in the center. Suspension is by a pair of gold wings. The ribbon is blue 3mm, white 2½mm, blue 7mm, light blue 11mm, blue 7mm, white 2½mm, blue 3mm.

Background: Just as with the Air Force DSO, which is identical to this medal except for the metal colors, Vietnamese-made versions vary in size and detail. The US-made version closely resembles a Vietnamese-made one (and has light blue paint behind the jet planes), but has on the reverse the inscription *VIỆTNAM* in a neat-lined circle.

Rarity: R-5

Vietnamese

14 NAVY MERITORIOUS SERVICE MEDAL
Hải-Quân Vinh-Công Bội-Tinh — **June 5, 1964**

Purpose: For NCO's and enlisted men of the Navy for citations and wounds in combat or line of duty, or exceptional achievements that reflect great credit on or benefit to the Navy in any field.

Description: Front: a gold Maltese cross with engraved lines and indented slightly along the center of the rays and in the center a white disk with a silver compass rose surrounded by a blue ribbon with marks for the eight compass directions, and surrounded again with a yellow ribbon with the inscription above *HẢI-QUÂN* and below *VINH-CÔNG*, with three small red lines before and behind the two inscriptions, 36mm. Back: stamped *VIỆTNAM* in a lined circle. The ribbon is blue 5mm, green 3½mm, blue 7mm, white 5½mm, blue 7mm, green 3½mm, blue 5mm.

Background: The originally produced versions of this were better made and larger, 38mm in diameter. The US-made version has a fixed suspension integral to the casting and has neater enamel. The design seems to be a ship's wheel enclosing a compass rose. It was authorized for award to allied enlisted personnel.

Rarity: R-4

Vietnamese

15 SPECIAL SERVICE MEDAL
Biệt-Công Bội-Tinh — **May 12, 1964**

Purpose: For military personnel, government employees and civilians who distinguished themselves in extraordinary deeds or accomplished an important mission that involved risk of life and required exceptional fortitude and aggressiveness — generally of a clandestine nature. Also presented to foriegn military personnel serving by the side of RVN units. Five combat missions north of the 17th parallel qualified RVN personnel for this medal.

Description: Front: silver eight-pointed star, 40mm, with central planchet enameled black, with a hand holding a dagger pointing down in silver, surrounded with silver ribbon inscribed above *BIỆT-CÔNG BỘI-TINH*; Back: stamped *VIỆT-NAM* in a lined circle. The ribbon is red 4mm, white 4mm, red 4mm, white 4mm, red 4mm, white 4mm, red 4mm, white 4mm, red 4mm. The device worn is a miniature representation of the medal, worn on both the ribbon suspension and also on the service bar.

Background: This was intended as a reward for spooky missions, and probably was never authorized by our authorities for receipt and wear by Americans. A manufacturer's variant has been made with seven red and six white stripes on the ribbon. The US-made ribbon with bound edge is notably different: red 6½mm, white 3mm, red 3mm, white 3mm, red 3mm, white 3mm, red 3mm, white 3mm, red 6½mm. The US-made version of the badge has a fixed suspension, is quite flat and slightly cartoonish in appearance, and has a plain back.

Rarity: R-5

Ameican *Vietnamese*

16 GALLANTRY CROSS
Anh-Dũng Bội-Tinh/Croix de la Vallance
four grades — August 15, 1950

Purpose: For valor or heroic conduct while fighting the enemy.

Description: Front: bronze, a cross patee, with the four arms interconnected by engraving representing two dragons, and with two crossed sabres between the arms, handles down, and with a disk in the center with the map of Vietnam with a laurel branch on either side and the ribbon across inscribed *QUỐC-GIA LAO-TƯỞNG* (Reward of the State), 47mm; Back: same as design on front except disk in center plain. Suspension is by a rectangular shape of two dragons facing each other. The ribbon is red 10mm, yellow 16mm, with eight pairs of thread-like red stripes 1mm apart, red 10mm.

Palm
Purpose: For citation at the Army or Armed Forces level.
Description: There is a large bronze palm device on the suspension ribbon and a small one on the service bar. The original regulations specified two crossed palm leaves. A blackened palm was reportedly used late in the war for posthumous awards. A silver palm was sometimes used for five bronze palms.

Gold Star
Purpose: For citation at the Corps level.
Description: The device is a gold star, rather large.

Silver Star
Purpose: For citation at the Division level.
Description: The device is a silver star.

Bronze Star
Purpose: For citation at the Brigade and Regiment level.
Description: The device is a bronze star.

Unit Award (*Huy-Hiệu Tuyên-Công Đơn-Vị*).
Description: The ribbon is in a gold frame with a leaf pattern, with the four devices by grade as above.

Background: This equivalent of the French Croix de Guerre was at first sparingly given, but as the war continued was widely bestowed — although often, for the infantrymen, a reward for much heroism and peril. Some soldiers had received so many Gallantry Crosses that they would wear their cross with a long, device-covered suspension ribbon and several of the ribbons all covered with the devices in their service bar sets. The Gallantry Cross could be presented on the spot to deserving soldiers by the regimental commander or province chief without the preliminary paperwork required with most other awards. This was also a blackened version of the Gallantry Cross reportedly with palm given as a posthumous award to the relatives of soldiers killed in action.

Many American servicemen received the Cross of Gallantry either as a personal award or as a unit award. Just as the French generously bestowed the Croix de Guerre in World Wars I and II on their allies, so did the South Vietnamese extensively award the Gallantry Cross to the Americans and other allies in their war.

Vietnamese-made versions vary much in quality. French-made versions are heavier and well made. One US-made version has the tips of the sabres straight, the heads of the dragons reduced to a few lines, and the arms of the cross with a small plain margin between the thin edge rim and the pebbled design. US-made palms and stars are sometimes much smaller than Vietnamese and French-made palms and star devices. A Japanese-made Gallantry Cross is of a brassy metal, with the ribbon in the center mistakenly reading *KQUỐC GIA LAO-TƯỞNG*.

Rarity: R-1

French Croix de Guerre   *Vietnamese*   *Ameican*   *Vietnamese*   *Ameican*

17 AIR GALLANTRY CROSS
Phi-Dũng Bội-Tinh
three grades —

Purpose: For display of heroism and exceptional bravery in flight or in extremely dangerous situations. Awarded to RVN Air Force personnel, civilian flying personnel serving in the Air Force and allied flying personnel.

Description: Front: Maltese cross in silver with the center of the arms indented and with stylized gold jet planes in the corners of the arms, and in the center a blue disk with a silver star within two thin silver circles, 40mm; Back: stamped *VIỆT-NAM* in a lined circle with the inscription around *PHI-DŨNG BỘI-TINH*. Suspension is by a pair of gold wings. The ribbon is grey 12mm, blue 12mm, grey 12mm.

Gold Wing
Purpose: For citation at Air Force level.
Description: The device is gold stylized wings and star.
Silver Wing
Purpose: For citation at Tactical Wing level.
Description: The device is silver stylized wings and star.
Bronze Wing
Purpose: For citation at Squadron level.
Description: The device is bronze stylized wings and star.

Background: The US-made version is a close copy of the Vietnamese-made one except that the central star is affixed instead of being a part of the cast design. Early made Air Gallantry Crosses are appreciably larger. Illustrations of the initial design picture a device on the ribbon like the central disk of the medal. The Vietnamese-made wing and star devices vary in size.

Rarity: R-3

18 NAVY GALLANTRY CROSS
Hải-Dũng Bội-Tinh
three grades — June 5, 1964

Purpose: For servicemen of the Navy for coolness and heroism while the vessel was underway and in distress due to a technical failure, foul weather or combat.

Description: Front: cross-like four spear points with smaller pointed and lined rays between, in gold, with central disk of blue with anchor and Vietnamese national flag design shield, surrounded with ribbon with inscription *HẢI-DŨNG BỘI-TINH,* 37mm. Back: the inscription *VIỆTNAM* in a lined circle with a rim of thin lines radiating outwards. The ribbon is blue 12mm, white 12mm, blue 12mm.

Gold Anchor or First Class
Description: The device is a gold anchor on both the suspension ribbon and service bar.
Silver Anchor or Second Class
Description: The device is a silver anchor on both the suspension ribbon and service bar.
Bronze Anchor or Third Class
Description: The device is a bronze anchor on both the suspension ribbon and service bar.

Background: The US-made version is flattish and has a fixed suspension, rather large lettering, and neater, if scrawnier looking, enamel work in the center. The US-version sometimes comes with ribbon with unbound edges. The anchors designated the citation level similar to the Gallantry Cross. It was also intended for civilian and allied personnel with the Navy.

Rarity: R-4

19 HAZARDOUS SERVICE MEDAL
Ưu-Dũng Bội-Tinh - June 5, 1964

Purpose: For display of heroism in the protection of government property or the life of government officials, or for having long-endured danger in order to accomplish a strategic mission in a remote area under constant enemy threat, or for having proved enthusiasm and determination in the accomplishment of a dangerous mission not involving direct participation in combat. Awarded to both Vietnamese and allies.

Description: Front: Maltese cross in gold with the center of the arms indented, and in the center, a yellow disk with a silver star within two thin gold circles, and the inscription *UU-DŨNG* above and *BỘI-TINH* below within the disk, 38mm; Back: the inscription *VIỆT-NAM* a lined circle with a rim of thin lines radiating outwards. The ribbon is blue 5mm, red 5mm, blue 5mm, red 5mm, blue 5mm, red 5mm, blue 5mm. The device is a small silver palm leaf, for each award.

Background: the US-made version is a close copy, but with neater workmanship and brighter metal; the design and inscription on the reverse are the same, but are small.

Rarity: R-5

20 LIFE SAVING MEDAL
Nhân-Dũng Bội-Tinh — May 12, 1964

Purpose: For extreme bravery in risking life to rescue other people in distress.

Description: Front: in the center, a red cross with the base of the arms somewhat thicker, inside a similarly shaped white border, and on a gold-bordered cross of the same shape, 36mm; Back: stamped in three lines *NHÂN-DŨNG BỘI-TINH VIỆT-NAM*. The ribbon is red 3mm, white 2mm, red 10mm, white 7mm, red 10mm, white 2mm, red 3mm.

Background: This was for civilians as well as military personnel. The Vietnamese-made version is slightly concave, while the US-made one is flat and has on the reverse the inscription *VIỆTNAM* in a lined circle. One Vietnamese manufacturer's variety has the cross bordered in red. It was awarded to allies who rescued Vietnamese citizens. Australians who received this award were allowed to wear it in uniform.

Rarity: R-5

21 LOYALTY MEDAL
Trung-Chánh Bội-Tinh — May 12, 1964

Purpose: For loyalty to the National Cause evidenced through denouncing and countering enemy subversive activities that are prejudicial to the security and order of the country.

Description: Front: thin-pointed gold star with pieces between the points resembling blunt spear points in gold, and on a central gold disk the inscription *TRUNG* (loyalty) in the form of a T above R on the left, a high U in the center, and an N above G on the right, 39mm; Back: stamped with the inscription *TRUNG-CHÁNH BỘI-TINH VIỆT-NAM* in a circle with a small four-pointed star in the center. The ribbon is white 12mm, red 12mm, white 12mm. At times, the medal has the device of a silver palm.

Background: The US-made version closely resembles the Vietnamese-made one except the reverse has the inscription *VIỆT-NAM* in a lined circle. The pattern of the *TRUNG* in the center is an example of how the Vietnamese sometimes grouped the alphabet to appear as a Chinese character.

Rarity: R-5

22 WOUND MEDAL
Chiến-Thương Bội-Tinh — January 3, 1953

Purpose: For military personnel who had been wounded in action and to government officials wounded in the line-of-duty by the enemy or rebels.

Description: Front: a red six-pointed star, with small balls on the points, and with a gold grasslike design and tiny fleur-de-lis between the points, and a gold fleur-de-lis on the uppermost point, 35mm. Back: in a semicircle at the top an inscription, and below in three lines *CHIẾN-THƯƠNG BỘI-TINH*. The ribbon is white 1½mm, light green 4mm, white 1½mm, light green 1½mm, white 1½mm, yellow 6mm, red 3mm, yellow 6mm, white 1½mm light green 1½mm, white 1½mm, light green 44mm, white 1½mm. Device is a red star for each award.

Version of the State of Vietnam
Description: Inscription on top back reads *QUỐC-GIA VIỆT-NAM*.

Version of the Republic of Vietnam
Description: Inscription on top back reads *VIỆT-NAM CỘNG-HÒA*.

Background: Both the medal and ribbon closely resemble the French equivalent Médaille des Blessés Militaires. This medal is for servicemen and civil officials. The French-made version of this medal of the State of Vietnam is better made than the Vietnamese-made version. The US-made version of the Wound Medal of the Republic of Vietnam has a more delicate appearance and a plain reverse. Americans wounded in Vietnam, of course, received instead the Purple Heart.

Rarity: State of Vietnam R-3; Republic of Vietnam R-2

23-24 ARMED FORCES HONOR MEDAL
Danh-Dự Bội-Tinh — two classes — January 7, 1953

Purpose: For contributions to the formation and organization of the Armed Forces and the training of troops and technical cadres of the various branches. It was intended for non-combat achievements.

Description: Front: a cross formee couped with additional points reflected down the arms and with thin blade points coming between the arms, and in the central disk, a coiled dragon with a ribbon around inscribed above *DANH-DỰ BỘI-TINH* and below *VIỆT-NAM*, with a wreath of oak leaves around the design of the cross arms, 38mm. Back: plain. Suspension is by a laurel wreath.

23 First Class
Purpose: For officers.
Description: Above in gold. The ribbon is yellow 1½mm, red 6mm, yellow 3mm, light blue 3mm, yellow 3mm, light blue 3mm, yellow 3mm, light blue 3mm, yellow 3mm, red 6mm, yellow 1½ mm. Device on the service bar is a gold eagle with shield on breast and holding swords.

24 Second Class
Purpose: For NCO's and enlisted men.
Description: Above in silver. The ribbon is 7½mm, yellow 3mm, light blue 3mm, yellow 3mm, light blue 3mm, yellow 3mm, light blue 3mm, yellow 3mm, red 7½mm. Device on the service bar is a silver eagle with shield on its breast and holding swords.

Armed Forces Honor Medal continued

Armed Forces Honor Medal First Class Vietnamese

Armed Forces Honor Medal First Class American

Armed Forces Honor Medal Second Class Vietnamese

Armed Forces Honor Medal Second Class American

Armed Forces Honor Medal with devices Vietnamese

Armed Forces Honor Miniature Medals American Made

Background: This was widely conferred on American officers and men who wore it without a ribbon device. This early award of the State of Vietnam was originally entitled in French, La Médaille du Merite Vietnamien, and was intended in part under the decree for "French or foreign military men who participated, in the capacity of advisors, in the working out of the Vietnamese military legislation and regulations" or "French or foreign military men who directly contributed to the raising and organizing of the units of the National Army." The original decree specified a ribbon width of 34mm. The French-made version (and some Vietnamese copies) have a prominent rectangular bar for the ribbon behind the suspension wreath, and have raised lettering on the ribbon around the central disk rather than indented lettering. A US-made version closely resembles the Vietnamese-made one. A small difference in one make is the absence of the few dot-like clouds around the central dragon that are seen on the Vietnamese and French-made versions. Another US-made version has a suspension wreath of a flat, slightly cartoonish laurel wreath.

Rarity: First Class R-2; Second Class R-2

25 LEADERSHIP MEDAL
Chỉ-Đạo Bội-Tinh
seven grades — June 5, 1964

Purpose: For commanders of combat units (company and above) who have displayed excellent leadership in combat operations, training, troop discipline and morale over two-years duty.

Description: Front: four-pointed gold star, 40mm, crossed by swords, and backed by green-enameled round wreath; Back: stamped with a lined square diamond with inscription inside *VIỆT-NAM* and around the four edges *CHỈ-ĐẠO BỘI-TINH*. The ribbon is green 3mm, white 11mm, pink 9mm, white 11mm, green 3mm.

First Grade
Purpose: For Armed Forces commander's award.
Description: Device is a gold-edged yellow rectangle 10mm by 5mm with five X's above.
Second Grade
Purpose: For corps commander's award.
Description: Device is the same with three X's above.
Third Grade
Purpose: For division commander's award.
Description: Device is the same with two X's above.
Fourth Grade
Purpose: For brigade commander's award
Description: Device is the same with one X above.
Fifth Grade
Purpose: For regiment commander's award.
Description: Device is the same with three I's above.
Sixth Grade
Purpose: For battalion commander's award.
Description: Device is the same with two I's above.
Seventh grade
Purpose: For company commander's award.
Description: Device is the same with one I above.

Background: This was originally intended to spur competition for unit improvement, but it is basically a good conduct award for commanding officers, the devices going by rank. For instance, a four-star general would get the first grade, three-star—the second grade, and down accordingly by command rank. The device, supposedly worn on both the suspension ribbon and the service bar, is the unit symbol in military mapping. In practice, however, this device was seldom worn on either the medal ribbon or the bar, so it was not possible to tell the grade of the award. The regulations allowed up to three devices on the ribbon. The US-made version closely resembles the Vietnamese-made ones, except it has better enamel in the wreath and has on the back the inscription *VIỆT-NAM* in a small lined circle.

Rarity: R-3

26 STAFF SERVICE MEDAL
Tham Mưu Bội-Tinh
two classes — May 12, 1964

Purpose: For staff service to the Armed Forces evidencing outstanding initiative and devotion to duty.

Description: Front: a square fortress design, with bastions at each point, suspended from one point, with a sword and writing brush crossing underneath, and in the center a blue diamond with gold crossed rifles, wings and anchor symbol of the Armed Forces, 40mm. Back: stamped in a circle THAM-MUU BỘI-TINH VIỆT-NAM with a tiny four-pointed star in the center.

First Class
Purpose: For officers.
Description: The ribbon is green 3mm, diagonal red 7mm and white 3mm stripes 30mm, green 3mm.

Second Class
Purpose: For NCO's and enlisted men.
Description: The ribbon is blue 3mm, diagonal red 7mm and white 3mm stripes 30mm, blue 3mm.

Background: This was widely given to American advisors. The US-made version closely resembles the Vietnamese-made ones; one small detail of difference is that the sword and pen of the US-made one has a more squarish shape in contrast to the more sculptured shape of the Vietnamese-made one. The US-made ones have the same reverse design, except neater. One noticeable difference with the US-bound edge ribbon is that it usually has a thin black stripe — which the Vietnamese ribbon does not have — between the blue or green edge and the red and white diagonals. It normally required at least six months duty with a Vietnamese unit for award to allied personnel. It is also occasionally referred to as the Staff Service Honor Medal.

Rarity: First Class R-2; Second Class R-2

27 TECHNICAL SERVICE MEDAL
Kỹ-Thuật Bội-Tinh
two classes — June 5, 1964

Purpose: For military servicemen and civilians working as military technicians who have shown outstanding professional capacity, initiative, and devotion to duty.

Description: Front: gold, four aircraft propeller blades, 50mm across, interspersed with four ship's propeller blades, and between those eight white enameled rays, inside a planchet shaped as a gear, and in the center on a blue-green background—the Armed Forces insignia of wings, crossed rifles, and an anchor. Back: a stamped-lined circle inscribed inside VIỆT-NAM and around the edge KỸ-THUẬT BỘI-TINH.

First Class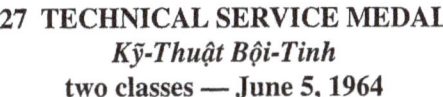
Purpose: For officers.
Description: The ribbon is silver grey 5mm, red 2mm, silver grey 20mm, red 2mm, silver grey 5mm, and in the center two thread-like red stripes 1mm apart.

Second Class
Purpose: For NCO's and enlisted men.
Description: The ribbon is the same except without the two thread-like red stripes in the center.

Background: This was also frequently awarded to American advisors. The US-made version closely resembles the Vietnamese-made ones except that it has a fixed suspension, is slightly flatter, and has brighter gold and neater paint. It is occasionally called the Technical Services Honor Medal.

Rarity: First Class R-2; Second Class R-2

28 TRAINING SERVICE MEDAL
Huấn-Vụ Bội-Tinh
two classes — May 12, 1964

Purpose: For instructors and cadres at military schools and training centers and civilians and foreigners who contribute significantly to training.

Description: Gold rectangle, 20mm wide and 50mm high. Front: sword surmounted with open book and with inscription *HUẤN-VỤ BỘI-TINH* at bottom. Back: stamped with a lined diamond with inscription *HUẤN-VỤ BỘI-TINH* along the sides and *VIET-NAM* in center.

First Class
Purpose: For officers.
Description: The ribbon is white 3mm, pink 9mm, white 11mm with two thread-like pink stripes 1mm apart in center, pink 9mm, white 3mm.
Second Class
Purpose: For NCO's and enlisted men.
Description: The ribbon is the same as the First Class, but without the two thread-like pink stripes in the center.

Background: The US-made version closely resembles the well-made Vietnamese-made ones except it has a less sculptured look, the pebbling is slightly larger, and the reverse is plain. It is occasionally called the Training Service Honor Medal.

Rarity: First Class R-3; Second Class R-3

29 CIVIL ACTIONS MEDAL
Dân-Vụ Bội-Tinh
two classes — May 12 1964

Purpose: For outstanding achievements in the field of civil affairs.

Description: Front: eight-pointed gold star, with the points on the diagonal being smooth and long and the points on the horizontal and vertical being a little shorter and with cut lines, and in the center a brown disk with the figure of a soldier, a child, and a farmer with a shovel, surrounded with a white ribbon inscribed above *DÂN-VỤ* and below *BỘI-TINH* with many short lines between, 30mm. Back: plain.

First Class
Purpose: For officers.
Description: The ribbon is green 2mm, red 5mm, green 22mm with two thin thread-like red stripes in center 1mm apart, red 5mm, green 2mm.
Second Class
Purpose: For NCO's and enlisted men.
Description: The ribbon is the same but without the two thread-like red stripes in center.
Unit Award (*Huy-Hiệu Tuyên-Công Đơn-Vị*)
Description: The ribbon is the same as for the First Class. It is in a gold frame with a leaf pattern.

Background: Particularly as a unit award, this was widely bestowed on the American forces in Vietnam. One US-made version closely resembles the Vietnamese-made ones except that the central disk is higher, the enamel neater, the gold brighter, and the reverse plain. It is occasionally called the Civic Actions Honor Medal.

Rarity: First Class R-2; Second Class R-2

30 GOOD CONDUCT MEDAL
Quân-Phong Bội-Tinh — five grades — June 5, 1964

Purpose: For all ranks for at least three years of service and the display of exempla conduct and discipline with five years for position in grade.

Description: Front: six-rayed gold star, where the rays are like flattened spear points ar between them are cut lines extending to a balled point, and in the central disk two drago holding a shield with the three red stripes of the Vietnamese arms, with around a ribbon i scribed above *QUÂN-PHONG* and below *BỘI-TINH*, 38mm. Back: plain. The ribbon is lig blue 4mm, white 7mm, light blue 1½mm, white 1½ mm, red center 8mm, white 1½ mm, lig blue 1½ mm, white 7mm, light blue 4mm.

First Grade
Description: There are five silver fleur-de-lis devices.
Second Grade
Description: There are four silver fleur-de-lis devices.
Third Grade
Description: There are three silver fleur-de-lis devices.
Fourth Grade
Description: There are two silver fleur-de-lis devices.
Fifth Grade
Description: There is one silver fleur-de-lis device.

Background: The US-made version closely resembles the Vietnamese-made ones exce that the central Vietnamese shield is in well-done enamel and the reverse has the inscriptic *VIET-NAM* in a lined circle.

Rarity: R-4

31 CAMPAIGN MEDAL
Chiến-Dịch Bội-Tinh — May 12, 1964

Purpose: For participation in the military campaign in Vietnam.

Description: Front: a white six-pointed star with cut lined, broad gold star points between, and a central green disk with a map of Vietnam in silver surmounted with three painted flames in red, signifying the three regions of Vietnam, 38mm. Back: the inscription *VIỆT-NAM* in a lined circle with around *CHIẾN-DỊCH* above and *BỘI-TINH* below separated by many short lines. The ribbon is green 2mm, white 5mm, green 7mm, white center 6mm, green 7mm, white 5mm, green 2mm. The device is a silver ribbon 28mm lon~ on the suspension ribbon and 15mm long on the service bar usuall inscribed: "1960", (for most awards worn by allied soldiers). De vices are inscribed "1949-54" for Vietnamese who participated i the campaign then. For the devices on the ribbon bars the dates ar abbreviated "49-54" and "60". Apparently unofficial full-sized bar for medals are known with dates 1964, 1965, 1966, 1967; 1967-6! and 1969-70; ribbon bars devices are also known with various date:

Background: The governments of the allied forces in Vie nam authorized their personnel to receive this award from the Re public of Vietnam for six months service there (or for wounds c death in action). It was authorized for American service personne by DOD instruction 1348.19 of Jan. 31, 1974. The medal exis with many small variations by its extensive manufacture in Vie nam and abroad in the US, Japan, Korea and perhaps elsewherc Vietnamese-made versions usually are cast with a linked susper sion and a concave central disk, although stamped versions ar also known. One US-made version is flattish with fine ename and has slightly broader angled rays between the white arms of th star, a fixed suspension, and a raised inscription on the reverse

Another US-made version resembles this, except that the central disk is concave and is attached. The proper awards for Commonwealth personnel for Vietnam service are engraved with name, rank, and serial number following British practice. The original design for this medal was the same design on the central disk as the Army DSO, and had place named ribbon devices, perhaps marking individual battles.

Rarity: R-1 (dates other than 1960 - raise the rarity)

32 MILITARY SERVICE MEDAL
Quân-Vụ Bội-Tinh
five grades — May 12, 1964

Purpose: For completion of a prescribed service time and display of good conduct and high-working spirit.

Description: Front: in a cross patee form, four sets of white V's with the points in the center, surmounting a green wreath, and in the center a small cross patee with crossed swords, 37mm. Back: in a diamond shape, with inscription *QUÂN-VỤ BỘI-TINH* around, the horizontal inscription *VIỆT-NAM* with horizontal lines above and below (other reverse designs also). The ribbon is yellow 3½mm, green 5½mm, yellow 1mm, green 14mm, yellow 1mm, green 5½mm, yellow 3½mm.

First Grade
Purpose: For 23 years service.
Description: There are five small silver palm-leaf devices.
Second Grade
Purpose: For 18 years service.
Description: There are four small silver palm-leaf devices.
Third Grade
Purpose: For 13 years service.
Description: There are three small silver palm-leaf devices.
Fourth Grade
Purpose: For 8 years service.
Description: There are two small silver palm-leaf devices.
Fifth Grade
Purpose: For 3 years service.
Description: There is one small silver palm-leaf device.

Background: The US-made version closely resembles the Vietnamese-made ones except that it has fine enamel work and on the reverse the inscription *VIỆT-NAM* in a small lined circle.

Rarity: R-3

33 AIR SERVICE MEDAL
Không-Vụ Bội-Tinh
four grades — May 12, 1964

Purpose: For a prescribed number of flight hours.

Description: Front: a six pointed gold star with cut lines on the points, and in the center a light blue globe surmounted with a gold jet plane, 36 mm. Back: plain, or with stamped *VIỆT-NAM* in a lined circle with the inscription around *KHÔNG-VỤ BỘI-TINH*. Suspension is by a gold pair of wings.

First Grade
Purpose: For 1,000 flying hours.
Description: There is a small gold jet plane device on the suspension ribbon and service bar.
Second Grade
Purpose: For 600 flying hours.
Description: There is a small silver jet plane device.
Third Grade
Purpose: For 300 flying hours.
Description: There is a small bronze jet plane device.
Honor Grade (*Hạng Danh-Dự*)
Purpose: For honorary bestowal on a member of another service or a foreign serviceman for a worthy mission involving 10 flights on a RVNAF or allied aircraft.

33 AIR SERVICE MEDAL cont.

Description: There was a large wreath in gold, silver, or bronze. Or it is possible these may simply be for the above grades in a way done earlier, and the Honor Grade is simply without a device. Unfortunately, information on this is lacking.

Background: The categorization of the grades and devices is according to JGS/RVNAF Directive HT-655-425. The wreath devices for the suspension ribbon are quite large, about 22mm, but the jet plane devices are the same tiny ones used on the service bars. The US-made medals closely resembles the Vietnamese-made ones, except they have raised, instead of indented, lines of latitude and longitude and brighter gold. They have on the back the inscription VIỆT-NAM in a circle with CHIẾN-DỊCH BỘI-TINH (for the wrong medal!) and two sets of short lines around in a double-lined circle.

Rarity: R-3

First Version

34-35-36 NAVY SERVICE MEDAL
Hải-Vụ Bội-Tinh
four grades — May 12, 1964

Purpose: Awarded to RVNAF and allied personnel for completion of missions at sea for a certain period of time.

Description: The ribbon is light blue 4mm, dark blue 5mm, light blue 3½mm, white 10mm, light blue 3½mm, dark blue 5mm, light blue 4mm.

34 First Version
Description: Front: central disk of a stylized silver whale on blue waves and light blue sky on a gold compass rose which in turn is on a large silver anchor, 44mm. Back: plain.

35 Second Version
Description: Front: gold steering wheel surmounting a large gold anchor. Back: plain, or the inscription VIỆT-NAM in a lined circle with around HẢI-VỤ at the top and BỘI-TINH at the bottom separated by small stars of four points.

First Grade
Purpose: For 15 years service.
Description: The devices are a silver compass rose and two silver representations of three stylized waves.

Second Grade
Purpose: For 10 years service.
Description: The devices are two silver representations of three stylized waves.

Third Grade
Purpose: For 5 years service.
Description: The devices is a silver representation of three stylized waves.

Honor Grade
Purpose: For honorary bestowal on a member of another service.
Description: There are no devices.

Second Version

36 Third Version (apparently only manufactured in the US).
Description: Front: central disk of a stylized silver whale on blue waves and light blue sky, on a gold compass rose embellished with a silver wreath, and with a small gold anchor leading from the top of the compass rose to the suspension, 40mm. Back: inscribed VIỆT-NAM in a small lined circle.

Background: The third version is the one pictured in the official ARVN manual on medals, *Huy Chương Ân Thưởng Trong Quân-Lực Việt-Nam Cộng-Hòa,* but to the best of knowledge was not manufactured thus in Vietnam. The first version is the usual Vietnamese-made one, while the second version is rarer. The steering wheel of the second version looks closely like the Buddhist symbol of the "wheel of metempsychosis", and may have been a reason for the change of design. No authoritative source has been found on the devices, and the above information is open to question.

Rarity: First Version R-4; Second Version R-5; Third Version US made

Third Version

37 UNITY MEDAL
Nhất-Trí Bội-Tinh
May 12, 1964

Purpose: For civilians who have contributed to the development of the Armed Forces and who have been especially concerned about the material and spiritual welfare of the servicemen and their dependents.

Description: Front: six-pointed silver star whose rays are in the shape of spearpoints, with a central gold disk with a small cross patee with crossed swords, 34 mm. Back: stamped *VIỆT-NAM* in a lined circle with the inscription around *NHẤT-TRÍ BỘI-TINH* (also other reverses). The ribbon is yellow 3½mm, diagonal blue 6mm and white 4mm stripes 31mm, yellow 3½mm. The device consists of the gold wings, crossed rifles, and anchor symbol of the Armed Forces.

Background: The US-made versions closely resemble the Vietnamese-made ones except that the metal colors are brighter, the central disk is 16mm instead of 15mm, and the reverse has the inscription *VIỆT-NAM* in a lined circle. This medal was also reportedly presented to foreign civilians.

Rarity: R-6

38 MEDAL OF SACRIFICE
Vị-Quốc Bội-Tinh
May 12, 1964

Purpose: For the next of kin of military personnel and government officials who have lost their lives in the line of duty.

Description: Front: gold Maltese cross with indented center to the arms and green palm leaves between the arms, with a white disk with the wings, crossed rifles and anchor symbol of the Armed Forces in silver, surrounded with a blue ribbon inscribed *VỊ-QUỐC BỘI-TINH*, 37mm. Back: stamped *VIỆT-NAM* in a lined circle. The ribbon is red 2mm, violet 32mm, red 2mm (or red 3mm, reddish violet 29mm, red 3mm). The device is supposedly a gold palm leaf.

Background: This was not intended for wear by military personnel. The US-made version closely resembles the Vietnamese-made ones except that the medal is flattish rather than lightly concave and the wings, crossed rifles and anchor symbol of the Armed Forces are in gold. The official ARVN manual on medals pictures the Medal of Sacrifice with a gold palm-leaf device on both the suspension ribbon and the service bar, but the medal was sold, and probably thus presented, without the device.

Rarity: R-5

39 MEDAL FOR CAMPAIGNS OUTSIDE THE FRONTIER
Chiến-Trường Ngoại-Biên Bội-Tinh
ca. 1973

Purpose: For participation in campaigns in Cambodia and Laos.

Description: Front: a cross barby of four arrow points, half blue and half light blue, with a central disk of brown with the map of Vietnam in gold between two gold palm and branches, 38mm. Back: stamped *V.N.C.H.* in a lined circle with inscription *CHIẾN-TRƯỜNG NGOẠI-BIÊN BỘI-TINH* around. The ribbon is blue 3mm, white 2mm, blue 26mm, white 2mm, blue 3mm. The device is a silver rectangular plate, either cast or stamped, inscribed *KAMPUCHEA* for service in Cambodia and *HẠ-LÀO* for service in lower Laos.

Background: A US-made version of this apparently does not exist. This was the last new ARVN medal that was authorized. The four arrows of the design presumably symbolized the ARVN's determination to go outside its country's borders as necessary.

Rarity: R-6

40 AIR FORCE NORTHERN EXPEDITIONARY MEDAL
Không-Quân Bắc-Tiến Bội-Tinh
Feb. 1, 1966

Purpose: For flying personnel or Air Force groups or foreigners who have enthusiastically participated in air raids over North Vietnam north of the 17th parallel.

Description: Front: three lightning bolts, converging at bottom, surrounded by a wreath, in brass, 34mm. Back: plain, suspension of two small wings. The suspension ribbon and the service bar are horizontally divided with top-half red and bottom-half yellow. The device is a gold spear with point upwards, smaller on the service ribbon.

Background: This medal was authorized by Decree 032-a/CT/LDQC/SL of the National Leadership Council signed by the Chairman, Lt. Gen. Nguyen Van Thieu. It appears as if this was a legal award, and the few authentic examples of the medal known may just reflect the very few sorties the VNAF made over the north. The Vietnamese-made medal is of flat thin stamped brass, with the suspension of two small wings like that on other Vietnamese Air Force medals. An American-made version looks quite different, well made, solid, concave, with a number of small design differences, including an elongated suspension bar at the top of the badge and rather truncated looking suspension. The ribbon has a white painted arrow.

Rarity: R-10 (Vietnamese-made)

Vietnamese made   American made

**PROCEDURE FOR WEARING
REPUBLIC OF VIETNAM MEDALS
FOR CIVILIANS**

Republic of Vietnam Civilian Medals

National Order of Vietnam	Bảo-Quốc Huân-Chương
Kim Khanh Medal	Kim-Khánh
Chuong My Medal	Chương-Mỹ Bội-Tinh
Administrative Service Medal	Hành-Chánh Bội-Tinh
Dedicated Service Medal	Nghĩa-Vụ Bội-Tinh
Justice Medal	Tư-Pháp Bội-Tinh
Cultural and Educational Service Medal	Bội-Tinh Văn-Hóa Giáo Dục
Public Health Service Medal	Y-Tế Bội-Tinh
Social Service Medal	Xã-Hội Bội-Tinh
Economic Service Medal	Kinh-Tế Bội-Tinh
Finance Service Medal	Bội-Tinh Tài-Chánh
Psychological Warfare Medal	Bội-Tinh Tâm Lý-Chiến
Agricultural Service Medal	Nông-Nghiệp Bội-Tinh
Public Works, Communication & Transportation Service Medal	Bội-Tinh Công-Chánh và Giao-Thông Vận-Tải
Labor Medal	Lao-Động Bội-Tinh
Rural Revolutionary Development Medal	Xây-Dựng Nông-Thôn Bội-Tinh
Ethnic Development Service Medal	Bội-Tinh Phát-Triển Sắc-Tộc
Veterans Medal	Cựu-Chiến Binh Bội-Tinh
Police Merit Medal	Cảnh-Sát Chiến-Dự Bội-Tinh
Police Honor Medal	Cảnh-Sát Danh-Dự Bội-Tinh
People's Self-Defense Medal	Bội-Tinh Nhân-Dân Tự Vệ
Youth and Sports Service Medal	Bội-Tinh Thanh-Niên Thể Thao
Hamlet Common Defense Medal*	Bội-Tinh Toàn-Dân Bảo-Vệ Nôn-Song

* believed obsolete with the fall of Diem

Kim Khanh Decoration **pg. 55**

Sash and Badge Exceptional Class

First Class   Third Class   Second Class

Plate 8

45. Chuong My First Class **pg. 57**

46. Chuong My Second Class **pg. 57**

47. Administrative Service Medal First Class **pg. 57**

48. Administrative Service Medal Second Class **pg. 57**

49. Dedicated Service Medal First Class **pg. 58**

50. Dedicated Service Medal Second Class **pg. 58**

51. Justice Medal First Class **pg. 58**

52. Justice Medal Second Class **pg. 58**

Plate 9

53. Cultural and Educational Service Medal First Class **pg. 59**
54. Cultural and Educational Service Medal Second Class **pg. 59**
55. Public Health Service Medal First Class **pg. 59**
56. Public Health Service Medal Second Class **pg.59**

57. Social Service Medal First Class **pg. 60**
58. Social Service Medal Second Class **pg.60**
59. Economic Service Medal First Class **pg. 60**
60. Economic Service Medal Second Class **pg. 60**

Plate 10

61. Finance Service Medal First Class **pg. 61**
62. Finance Service Medal Second Class **pg. 61**
63. Psychological Warfare Medal First Class **pg. 61**
64. Psychological Warfare Medal Second Class **pg. 61**

65. Agricultural Service Medal First Class **pg. 62**
66. Agricultural Service Medal Second Class **pg. 62**

Public Works, Communications and Transportation Medals
67. First Class **pg. 62** 68. Second Class

Plate 11

69. Labor Medal First Class **pg. 63**

70. Labor Medal Second Class **pg. 63**

71. Labor Medal Third Class **pg. 63**

72. Rural Revolutionary Development Medal **pg. 63**

73. Ethnic Development Medal First Class **pg. 64**

74. Ethnic Development Medal Second Class **pg. 64**

75. Veterans Medal First Class **pg. 64**

76. Veterans Medal Second Class **pg. 64**

Plate 12

77. Police Merit Medal
First Class **pg. 65**

78. Police Merit Medal
Second Class **pg. 65**

79. Police Merit Medal
Third Class **pg. 65**

80. Police Honor Medal
First Class **pg. 66**

81. Police Honor Medal
Second Class **pg. 66**

82. Police Honor Medal
Third Class **pg. 66**

Plate 13

83. *People's Self-Defense Medal First Class* **pg. 67**
84. *People's Self-Defense Medal Second Class* **pg. 67**
85. *Youth and Sports Medal First Class* **pg. 67**
86. *Youth and Sports Medal Second Class*

87. *Presidential Unit Citation* **pg. 68**
88. *Civil Actions Unit Citation* **pg. 68**

89. *Gallantry Cross Unit Citations* **pg. 68**

90. *Police Merit Unit Citation* **pg.68**
91. *Police Honor Unit Citation* **pg. 68**

Examples of Vietnamese Miniature Medals

51

Plate 14

92. T'ai Federation Order of Civil Merit **pg. 70-71**

93. T'ai Federation Order of Military Merit **pg. 71**

94. Medal of the Nung Autonomous Zone **pg. 72**

95. Order of the Dragon of Annam Fourth Class **pg. 73**

96. French Croix de Guerre for Overseas Theaters of Operation **pg. 73**

97. French Colonial Medal **pg. 74**

98. French Indochina Medal **pg. 75**

99. French Wound Medal **pg. 75**

Plate 15

100. United States Vietnam Service Medal **pg. 77**

101. United States Service in Vietnam Award **pg. 78**

102. United States Armed Forces Expeditionary Medal **pg. 78**

103. United States Humanitarian Service Award **pg. 78**

104. Colorado National Guard Active Service Ribbon with clasp Vietnam Conflict **pg. 79**

110. Australian and New Zealand Vietnam Logistics and Support Ribbon **pg. 75**

105. United States Merchant Marine Vietnam Service Medal **pg. 79**

106. United States Commemorative Medal for Families of American Personnel Missing in Southeast Asia **pg. 79**

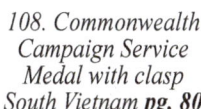

108. Commonwealth Campaign Service Medal with clasp South Vietnam **pg. 80**

109. Australian and New Zealand Vietnam Service Medal **pg. 81**

Plate 16

111. Republic of Korea Vietnam Participation Medal **pg. 82**

112. Thailand Vietnam Combat Service Medal **pg. 83**

113. Philippines Vietnam Service Medal **pg. 84**

114. Republic of China Memorial Medal of Honor for Vietnam **pg. 85**

115. International Commission for Supervision and Control 1967 Medal **pg. 86**

116. International Commission of Control and Supervision 1973 Medal with Second Version **pg. 87**

41-42-43-44 KIM KHANH DECORATION
Huy-Chương Kim-Khánh
four classes — Aug. 12, 1957

Purpose: Awarded or posthumously awarded to those Vietnamese citizens and foreign personalities who have distinguished themselves by exceptional achievements which helped develop human relations and understanding between peoples and between nations.

Description: The decoration is in the shape of a traditional Vietnamese gong (roughly butterfly shaped) in gold, the center having an open scholar's scroll with a writing brush on the left side and a sword on the right side, surmounted in the center with five stalks of bamboo with the leaves above and with curlicues below, and on either side a dragon with their heads on the middle of the upper right and left. Back and front are identical. The planchet is suspended by a thin pink cord which ends in a single bead and a green and yellow tassel. Suspended below, a bat-like design of beads, the body in red, the wings in yellow and outlined in light blue, and below that four red beads and then four small gold-lined cylinders, from each of which come five strings of beads alternately of five blue, yellow, orange, light green, and silver beads separated by three beads of white-blue-white ending in a tassel of threads. The service ribbon is blue 7mm, yellow 7mm, orange 7mm, light green 7mm, white 7mm, with slightly different colored devices attached.

41 Exceptional Class (*Đặc-Hạng*)
Description: Suspended from the neck, badge as above 90mm. Suspended from a sash, badge as above 75mm (sometimes a 60mm). Both neck badge and sash badge have bottom tassels of orange threads. Sash is orange, 100mm. The device on the service bar is a gold *Khánh* design with two ribands orange colored.

42 First Class (*Đệ-Nhất-Hạng*)
Description: Suspended from neck, badge as above 90mm. Badge has bottom tassels of yellow threads. Device on the service bar is a gold *Khánh* design with two ribands yellow colored.

43 Second Class (*Đệ-Nhị-Hạng*)
Description: Suspended from neck, badge as above 75mm. Badge has bottom tassels of light blue threads. Device on the service bar is a gold *Khánh* design with two ribands greenish-blue colored.

44 Third Class (*Đệ-Tam-Hạng*)
Description: Suspended from neck, badge as above 60mm. Badge has bottom tassels of purple threads. Device on the service bar is a gold *Khánh* design with two ribands blue colored.

Background: The government of President Diem revived the traditional *Khánh* as the second ranking award of the Republic, civil in character, although also awarded to senior military officers acting in a civil capacity. The *Khánh* (or *Kim Khánh*, the kim meaning gold) was an oriental-style award quite different from the other awards of the Republic which were based completely on western models.

The *Khánh* had the same name and shape as the Vietnamese stone or metal gongs which were used from ancient times for their pleasing sound and their ceremonial character. The *Khánh* was established as a distinction for high mandarins, sparingly bestowed and preserved with great pride in the family. The higher awards of the *Khánh* were initially often individually made with an inscription in Chinese characters chosen for special relevance to the honored recipient.

The *Khánh* was also made in jade for the emperor and reportedly at times in silver for low-ranking recipients. It was later standardized in a Great Class, plus First to Third Classes, in progressively smaller sizes. The design of the early *Khánh* were simple curlicues plus the inscription in Chinese characters. The *Khánh* of the later emperors up to Bao Dai had two dragons facing the sacred jewel and enclosing the inscription. They were generally made locally in Vietnam of two repousee gold pieces soldered together back to back. They also were made in both France and Vietnam of gilt silver or base metal in one piece.

The *Khánh* were hung from the neck by a simple red cord (or green cord, if the family was in mourning). Suspended below the *Khánh* would be an elaborate knot and tassels, often red, yellow, and green. On the later versions, the tassels consisted of beads in colored patterns.

The *Khánh* was only for men, and the equivalent for women was the Boi, an oblong piece in gold with a Chinese inscription and a design first of curlicues and later of phonenixes. It was also suspended by a cord and had an elaborate knot and tassels below.

The *Kim Khánh* of the Republic of Vietnam was presented in four classes, although the Exceptional Class had both a piece for suspension around the neck and a *Kim Khánh* on a large, orange-colored western-style sash. The new design had both the traditional dragons and a scholar's scroll, a fitting symbol for recipients who were comparable to the civil mandarins of earlier times. These *Kim Khánh* came in both cast, rather three-dimensional versions and quite flattish-looking stamped versions in all three sizes of badges. The ribbon for the service bar was not in orange, as the sash, but in the five colors that were apparently modeled on the colors of the beads in the tassels.

Rarity: Exceptional Class R-10; First Class R-8;   Second Class R-8; Third Class R-8

Older versions of the Khanh shown on this page (pre-RVN).

Kim Khanh Decoration

41 Exceptional Class (Đặc-Hạng)
Description: Suspended from the neck, badge as above 90mm. Suspended from a sash, badge as above 75mm (sometimes a 60mm). Both neck badge and sash badge have bottom tassels of orange threads. Sash is orange, 100mm. The device on the service bar is a gold *Khánh* design with two ribands orange colored.

42 First Class (Đệ-Nhất-Hạng)
Description: Suspended from neck, badge as above 90mm. Badge has bottom tassels of yellow threads. Device on the service bar is a gold *Khánh* design with two ribands yellow colored.

43 Second Class (Đệ-Nhị-Hạng)
Description: Suspended from neck, badge as above 75mm. Badge has bottom tassels of light blue threads. Device on the service bar is a gold *Khánh* design with two ribands greenish-blue colored.

44 Third Class (Đệ-Tam-Hạng)
Description: Suspended from neck, badge as above 60mm. Badge has bottom tassels of purple threads. Device on the service bar is a gold *Khánh* design with two ribands blue colored.

Sash and Badge Exceptional Class

First Class   *Second Class*   *Third Class*

45-46 CHUONG MY MEDAL
Chương-Mỹ Bội-Tinh
two classes — June 10, 1955

Purpose: Awarded or posthumously awarded to individuals or groups who distinguished themselves by sacrifices and courageous deeds, devotion to the service of the people, or glorious accomplishments in the cultural, economic and social fields.

Description: A saltire cross, 32mm across. Front: the rays of the cross are cleft, and in the angles between are small spear points with the suspension leading from the top ray of the four, and in the center a small rimmed plain disk. Back: plain, or in a small circle, *CHƯƠNG MỸ BỘI TINH*. The ribbon is a yellow 12mm, green 12mm, yellow 12mm.

45 First Class
Description: Rays of the cross are silver and the spear points and central disk are gold. The ribbon has a rosette on both the suspension ribbon and service bar.
46 Second Class
Description: Rays of the cross are gold (or tarnished brown) and the spear points and central disk are silver. The ribbon is without a rosette. The ribbon may also be in a size of 30mm.

Background: This was the third ranking civil order after the National Order and *Kim Khánh*. It could be awarded to military personnel (Article 122, Communique No. 47-NV dated September 5, 1955) who were performing civilian duties. It is a rather unimpressive looking award. The US-made version closely resembles the Vietnamese-made ones except that the badges for the two classes are in all gold and the back has in very small letters in a circle *CHƯƠNG MINH 408*.

Rarity: First Class R-5; Second Class R-6

47-48 ADMINISTRATIVE SERVICE MEDAL
Hành-Chánh Bội-Tinh
two classes — Mar. 18, 1967

Purpose: For members of the Administrative Service who distinguished themselves by length of service, efficiency, diligence, integrity, and good conduct; and for military personnel, members of specialized branches, private individuals or foreign nationals who render exceptional service to the Administrative Service.

Description: Front: diamond shape framed by two stylized palm leaves with inside a scholar's scroll on which is inscribed *HƯNG-QUỐC* (Build the Nation) and *AN DÂN* (Benefit the People), with below a ribbon inscribed *HÀNH-CHÁNH BỘI-TINH*, and above, between the ends of the palms, a small coin which leads to a fixed suspension in the shape of a stylized bat, 35mm. Back: inscribed *VIỆT-NAM*. The ribbon is blue 13mm, yellow 2mm, blue 5½mm, yellow 2mm, blue 13mm.

47 First Class
Description: Awarded in gold. On the service bar, but not on the suspension ribbon, there is a small gold scholar's scroll device (as in the center of medal).
48 Second Class
Description: Awarded in silver. On the service bar, but not on the suspension ribbon, there is a small silver scholar's scroll device.

Background: The scholar's scrolls are a traditional symbol of the literati and the mandarin. This would be given, for example, to a civilian deputy province chief. The bat is a traditional auspicious symbol in Vietnam and China.

Rarity: First Class R-5; Second Class R-5

49-50 DEDICATED SERVICE MEDAL
Nghĩa-Vụ Bội-Tinh
two classes — Mar. 18, 1967

Purpose: For civil servants and cadres of all services who distinguish themselves by great sacrifice and dedication while serving in dangerous areas.

Description: Front: six-pointed star with white points balled at the ends with forked rays between, with a central disk in green with a small shield in white with the inscription *TẬN-TỤY HY-SINH* (Devotion and Sacrifice) and two laurel branches on the side, surrounded with a yellow ribbon inscribed *NGHĨA-VỤ BỘI TINH* above and a series of short lines below, 38mm. Back: a circle inscribed in the center *VIỆT-NAM* with parallel lines above and below. The ribbon is yellow 12mm, red 12mm, yellow 12mm.

49 First Class
Description: Forked rays and edge of the medal in gold, as is the back. The device on the service bar is a small white shield with inscription as above and laurel branches on the sides in gold.

50 Second Class
Description: Forked rays and edge of the medal in dark bronze, as is the back. The device on the service bar is a small white shield with inscription as above and laurel branches in silver.

Background: This is slightly unusual in that the second class is bronze rather than silver.

Rarity: First Class R-5; Second Class R-5

51-52 JUSTICE MEDAL
Tư-Pháp Bội-Tinh
two classes — Apr. 21, 1967

Purpose: For civil servants and personnel in the judiciary for good conduct, positive and devoted service that brings honor to the nation's judiciary, and to others who contribute constructively and notably to the Judicial Branch.

Description: Front: two dragons with the sacred jewel between, 44mm, the ribbon below inscribed *TU-PHÁP*, and with a central disk with scales, open book, and upright sword encircled by a ribbon inscribed at top *LUẬT-PHÁP NHÂN-DÂN* (Law and the People), and below two palm leaves. Back: concave and plain. Suspension piece is a stylized bat. The ribbon is red 15mm, yellow 1½mm, blue 1½mm, yellow 1½mm, blue 1½mm, red 15mm.

51 First Class
Description: Awarded in gold. The device on the service bar, consists of scales, upright sword and an open book in gold.

52 Second Class
Description: Awarded in silver. The device on the service bar is as above in silver.

Background: The bat suspension is an auspicious symbol. The Justice Medal comes in an unusual number of manufacturer's variations. Some are stamped, and others cast in higher relief, on some with green paint highlighting. The central disk may be red encircled with green, white encircled in red, and perhaps other combinations. The varieties occur among a number of this medal bought in Saigon by Mr. Clement Kelly and appear to be examples of differences among manufacturers.

Rarity: First Class R-5; Second Class R-5

53-54 CULTURAL AND EDUCATIONAL SERVICE MEDAL
Bội-Tinh Văn-Hóa Giáo Dục
two classes — Aug. 1, 1968

Purpose: For teachers and civil servants of other cadres who have capably served the Cultural and Educational Branch, personnel of the Cultural and Educational Branch who have distinguished themselves by meritorious service or sacrificed their lives in the line of duty, or others who have distinguished themselves by meritorious service or by great sacrifice to the Cultural and Educational Branch.

Description: Oblong, 33mm — Front: green enameled palm leaves on left and magenta enameled leaves on right, with between a traditional building and below that a ribbon inscribed *VĂN-HÓA GIÁO-DỤC* with below that tied ribbons enameled yellow. Back: inscribed *VIỆT-NAM*. The ribbon is light green 4½mm, red 1¼mm, light green 1½mm, white 20mm, light green 1½mm, red 1¼mm, light green 4½mm.

53 First Class
Description: The central part of the design is gold. There is a rosette on the suspension ribbon and the service bar.

54 Second Class
Description: The central part of the design is silver. There is no rosette on the ribbon.

Background: The design is based loosely on that of the French Palmes Academiques, but with the old scholars hall added to the center.

Rarity: First Class R-5; Second Class R-3

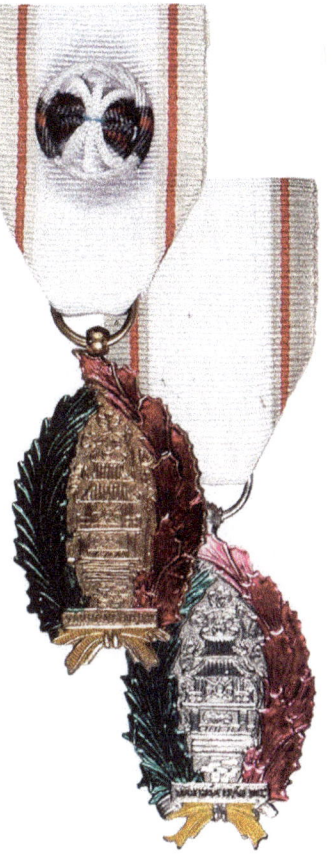

55-56 PUBLIC HEALTH SERVICE MEDAL
Y-Tế Bội-Tinh
two classes — Mar. 18, 1967

Purpose: For personnel of the Health Service who have displayed a sense of sacrifice and professional conscience when on duty, or citizens and civil servants not members of the Health Service for meritorious service in the development of national health, or physicians, dentists, pharmacists, nurses, and private individuals for extraordinary accomplishments during epidemics, and foreigners for meritorious service of benefit to public health in Vietnam.

Description: Front: a red Geneva cross with stylized leaves between the arms and a central disk in white with a stylized snake and staff encircled with a narrow red ribbon inscribed above *Y-TẾ BỘI-TINH* and around below with short lines, 37mm. Back: inscribed *VIỆT-NAM*. Suspension is a stylized leaf. The ribbon is yellow 1½mm, red 1mm, yellow 1½mm, white 28mm, yellow 1½mm, red 1mm, yellow 1½mm, and in the center a stripe of crenations of about 3mm, green on the left, red on the right, alternately 8mm and 4mm across.

55 First Class
Description: Stylized leaves between the arms and suspension device are in gold.
On the service bar, there is a device of a red Geneva cross, 6mm, with a stylized snake and staff in gold.

56 Second Class
Description: Stylized leaves between the arms and suspension device are in silver.
On the service bar, there is the same device with the stylized snake and staff in silver.

Background: The ribbon is distinctive and the red cross and caduceus identify it quickly as medical-related.

Rarity: First Class R-6; Second Class R-6

57-58 SOCIAL SERVICE MEDAL
Xã-Hội Bội-Tinh
two classes — June 10, 1967

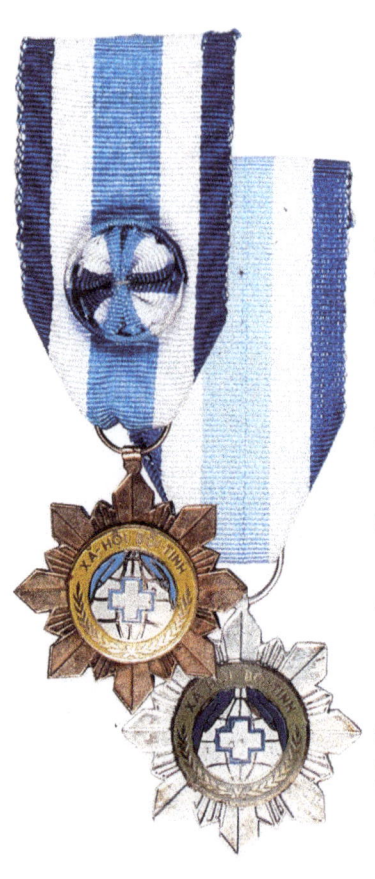

Purpose: For participation in social welfare activities in Vietnam.

Description: Front: star of eight-pointed rays (which are half indented) with smaller three-lined points between and a central disk of a white Geneva cross on a background design, encircled with a ribbon inscribed about *XÃ-HỘI BỘI-TINH*, and below with two palm leaves, 40mm. Back: inscribed *VIỆT-NAM*. The ribbon is blue 5mm, white 7mm, light blue center 12mm, white 7mm, blue 5mm either in large letters or more usually, in smaller letters.

Basic Version
Description: The background design of the central disk is light blue and white with a yellow ribbon.
Uncommon Version
Description: The background design of the central disk is red and gold or silver with a green ribbon.
57 First Class
Description: Star and inscription on the disk are in gold. The ribbon is supposed to be with a rosette on the suspension ribbon and service bar, but sometimes came without the rosette.
58 Second Class
Description: Star and inscription on the disk are in silver. There is no rosette on the ribbon.

Background: A number of American advisors who worked on refugee and other social issues received this. The American-manufactured version is close to the Vietnamese-made original, but has better quality enamel work on the central disk. The back is different by having *VIỆT-NAM* in a lined circle.

Rarity: First Class R-5; Second Class R-4

59-60 ECONOMIC SERVICE MEDAL
Kinh-Tế Bội-Tinh
two classes — Mar. 17, 1967

Purpose: For citizens or civil servants, legally established groups, administrative units that have distinguished themselves by meritorious service in commerce, industry, arts or crafts, or by inventions or initiatives that reflect credit on or are beneficial to the country. Also for persons in arts and crafts, industry, trade circles who have displayed great devotion to their occupations for over 10 years and have accomplished many meritorious achievements, or foreigners who have distinguished themselves in the development and growth of the national economy.

Description: Round, 36mm. Front: shocks of grain, two trunks of rubber trees with catching bowls, outline of factory with chimneys and smoke, with below a semicircular ribbon inscribed *KINH-TẾ BỘI-TINH*. Back: Inscribed *VIỆT-NAM* or plain. Suspension of leaves and berries. The ribbon is green 10mm, red 3mm, green 11mm, red 3mm, green 10mm.

9/1 First Class
Description: Awarded in gold. On the suspension ribbon in a 20mm size, and on the service bar in a 10mm size, there are devices of leaves and berries identical to the suspension piece, in gold.
9/2 Second Class
Description: Awarded in silver. Devices are in silver as above.

Background: This exists in stamped and cast manufacturers' versions which look notably different. It is roughly equivalent to the French and French Indochina Médaille du Travail given to loyal old workers. The design doubles in symbolism for both agriculture and industry.

Rarity: First Class R-5; Second Class R-5

61-62 FINANCE SERVICE MEDAL
Bội-Tinh Tài-Chánh
two classes — Nov. 11, 1968

Purpose: For personnel of the Finance Service who distinguish themselves by effectiveness, diligence, integrity, good conduct, meritorious service or sacrifice of their lives in the line of duty, and for others who distinguish themselves by meritorious service to the Finance Service.

Description: Front: star of five white cleft rays, each split down the middle with short balled points between the rays, and a central disk with dragon and several ancient coins and around a rim inscribed at the top BỘI-TINH TẢI-CHẮNH, 42mm. Back: a disk with a map of Vietnam, on the right a rising sun, on the left waves and above the inscription *VIỆT-NAM*. The ribbon is blue 7mm, white 4mm, blue 3mm, white 3mm, blue 3mm, white 3mm, blue 3mm, white 4mm, blue 7mm.

61 First Class
Description: Central disk and points between rays are in gold. The ribbon usually has a rosette on the suspension ribbon and the service bar.

62 Second Class
Description: Central disk and points between rays are in silver. There is no rosette.

Background: In accord with the usual manufacturer's varieties, this is also known with a simple reverse inscription *VIỆT-NAM*. One odd version of the First Class has the rays of the medal enameled in yellow. The traditional cash coins in the center naturally symbolize finance, as well as good fortune.

Rarity: First Class R-5; Second Class R-5

63-64 PSYCHOLOGICAL WARFARE MEDAL
Bội-Tinh Tâm-Lý-Chiến
two classes — Sept. 19, 1967

Purpose: For personnel and cadre of the Information and Open Arms Service who have 15 years of devoted service, have performed specially meritorious duty or have been wounded or sacrificed their lives in the line of duty, and for others who have contributed meritoriously to the Information or Open Arms Service.

Description: Front: a star of five megaphones, surmounted with lightning bolts, originating from the five petals of a yellow flower embellished with a green wreath, 35mm. Back: inscribed *VIỆT-NAM* and in a circle, *TÂM-LÝ-CHIẾN* above and *BỘI-TINH* below. Suspension is by a wreath. The ribbon is blue 3mm, white 7mm, blue 15mm, white 7mm, blue 3mm.

63 First Class
Description: Megaphones, central petals of the flower and suspension wreath in gold.
Device: On the service bar, there is a device in gold. (Devices are of two kinds: two megaphones from a pole on a round wreath, or a single megaphone on a wreath.)

64 Second Class
Description: Megaphones, central petals of the flower and suspension wreath in silver.
Device: On the service bar, there is a device in silver.

Background: This was awarded to a number of US officers who served as advisors to the Information and Open Arms Service. This, the *Chương My* Medal, and the Social Service Medal are the only civil awards of the Republic of Vietnam that were manufactured in the US. The US-made version is quite different from the Vietnamese-made version, being flat and stamped rather than cast and sculptured. The reverse is plain and the suspension wreath is round rather than oblong as on the Vietnamese-made version. Megaphones, of course, are an appropriate symbol for propaganda.

Rarity: First Class R-5; Second Class R-4

65-66 AGRICULTURAL SERVICE MEDAL
Nông-Nghiệp Bội-Tinh
two classes — Mar. 18, 1967

Purpose: For personnel of the Agricultural Service who have 15 years of devoted service, have performed specially meritorious duty, or have been wounded or sacrificed their lives in the line of duty, and for others who have contributed meritoriously to the Agricultural Service.

Description: Round, 35mm. Front: farmer wearing a conical straw hat, holding in his right hand a sheaf of rice, and in the left hand a hoe and sieve, with the head of a buffalo to the lower right of the medal and a thresher on the left with the inscription above *NÔNG-NGHIỆP BỘI-TINH*. Back: standing stalks of rice with below in small letters the inscription *VIỆT-NAM*. Suspension is by a small, plain, stylized bat. The ribbon is white 2mm, yellow 4½mm, very thin red-yellow 2mm, very thin red-yellow 4½mm, green 10mm, yellow 4½, very thin red-yellow 2mm, very thin red-yellow 4½mm, white 2mm.

65 First Class
Description: Awarded in gold. On the service bar, and sometimes on the suspension ribbon, there is a device of a sheaf of rice in gold.
66 Second Class
Description: Awarded in silver. On the service bar, and sometimes on the suspension ribbon, there is a device of sheaf of rice in silver.

Background: This exists in both stamped and cast manufacturer's versions. The pictured farmer wears the typical flat conical non la hat worn all over Vietnam.

Rarity: First Class R-5; Second Class R-5

67-68 PUBLIC WORKS, COMMUNICATIONS AND TRANSPORTATION SERVICE MEDAL
Bội-Tinh Công-Chánh và Giao-Thông Vận-Tải
two classes — Oct. 4, 1968

Purpose: For deserving civil servants who have had 15 years of continuous service in branches of the Public Works, Communications and Transportation Ministry, civil servants who have distinguished themselves by great benefit to the Service, or civil servants, Vietnamese citizens or foreigners who have distinguished themselves by exceptional service toward the implementation of Public Works, Communications and Transportation programs of genuine value in the technical or economic fields.

Description: Front: irregularly shaped design of a truck on a bridge, two standing plants, a canal, a railroad train, a ship, and at the top, a jet plane flying straight up, with the inscription at the bottom *CÔNG-CHÁNH GIAO-THÔNG VẬN-TẢI*, 29mm. Back: inscription *VIỆT-NAM*. The ribbon is red 8mm, white 1mm, yellow 1½mm, white 1mm, red 12½mm, white 1mm, yellow 1½mm, white 1mm, red 8mm.

67 First Class
Description: Awarded in gold. The ribbon has a rosette on suspension ribbon and service bar. The rosette in this case has a rim of alternating thin white and red stripes. Alternatively to the rosette on the suspension ribbon, there may be a metal device resembling the steering wheel of a vehicle in red, yellow and silver.
68 Second Class
Description: Awarded in silver. The ribbon has no rosette or device.

Background: This is certainly one of the most awkward and uninspired designs ever for a medal. The metal device is apparently correct for the suspension ribbon, but when the manufacturers ran out of them, they substituted the rosettes.

Rarity: First Class R-6; Second Class R-5

69-70-71 LABOR MEDAL
Lao-Động Bội-Tinh
two or three classes — Apr. 24, 1967

Purpose: For Vietnamese or foreign workers who have done well and distinguished themselves by devotion and sacrifice in their work in Vietnam, or Vietnamese and foreign persons and groups who have contributed meritorious service to national or international labor programs or civil servants and personnel of the Labor Service for good work and service with energy and devotion, or Vietnamese union members who contributed meritorious service to the realization of a labor program or policy of benefit to the growth of labor organizations and national development.

Description: Round, 38mm. Front: an anvil, two upright branches, two books on end, a kiln, and a row of rooftops, with above a thin circular line with the inscription *LAO-ĐỘNG BỘI-TINH*, and around the edge the teeth of a cogwheel. Back: inscription *VIỆT-NAM*; at the top a small triangular point leading to the suspension ring. The ribbon is light brown 10mm, yellow 2½mm, brown 10mm, yellow 2½mm, light brown 10mm.

69 First Class
Description: Awarded in gold. There is a rosette on the suspension ribbon and on the service bar.
70 Second Class
Description: Awarded in silver. The ribbon is without a rosette.
71 Third Class
Description: Awarded in bronze. The ribbon is without a rosette.

Background: The bronze medal was sold in Vietnam, but does not appear to have been officially authorized. It is not listed in the official awards and decorations books published in RVN in 1972.

Rarity: First Class R-5; Second Class R-5; Third Class R-4

72 RURAL REVOLUTIONARY DEVELOPMENT MEDAL
Xây-Dựng Nông-Thôn Bội-Tinh
Nov. 4, 1966

Purpose: For civilian or military personnel who actively contributed to, and sacrificed for the work of rural areas, or for Vietnamese groups, associations, citizens or foreigners and foreign groups that actively contributed to rural construction program.

Description: Front: an elongated gold triangle with curved designs on bottom corners and an edge of a repeated leaf pattern, and in the center a map of Vietnam in red and gold with the inscription at the apex *TỔ QUỐC* (fatherland) and at the bottom *NHÂN-DÂN* (people), and with a ribbon below inscribed *XÂY-DỰNG NÔNG-THÔN* (rural construction), 40mm. Back: plain: suspension is by a straight plain bar. The ribbon is dark brown 13½mm, yellow 10mm, dark brown 13½mm. The device is a gold palm leaf of the same shape as that for the Gallantry Cross, 35mm on suspension ribbon and 13mm on service bar.

Background: This was the only civil medal just in one class. The Americans liked to translate *XÂY-DỰNG NÔNG-THÔN* as "rural revolutionary development". A more accurate translation is "rural construction".

Rarity: R-5

73-74 ETHNIC DEVELOPMENT SERVICE MEDAL
Bội-Tinh Phát-Triển Sắc-Tộc
two classes — June 27, 1968

Purpose: For civilian and military personnel who worked with energy and devotion to produce excellent results in the improvement of the intellectual and material living standards of the ethnic minorities and for Vietnamese and foreign groups, associations and individuals who actively contributed to the improvement of the ethnic minorities.

Description: Front: native shield, inscribed at top PHÁT-TRIỂN SẮC-TỘC and crossed with bundle of arrows and quiver with a hand holding a torch, and, at top an x-like design leading to a fixed suspension, 35mm. Back: inscribed VIỆT-NAM. The ribbon is yellow 2mm, white 1mm, black 15mm, red 15mm, white 1mm, and yellow 2mm.

73 First Class
Description: Awarded in gold. The device is a silver elephant head in a ring, 18mm on the suspension ribbon and 9mm on the service bar.

74 Second Class
Description: Awarded in silver. The device is a silver elephant head without a ring around it.

Background: This exists in both cast and stamped manufacturer's versions. The minority highland peoples of Vietnam, the Montaguards or Dega, lived unfortunately in the areas worst impacted by the war. The minister for Ethnic Development was usually a minority highlander himself, and his ministry, with limited resources, tried to alleviate the many troubles of the minority peoples. The few remaining elephants in Vietnam were in the highland country of the Montaguards, and sometimes tamed and trained by them for transportation. The Montaguards gave an elephant as a gift to President Thieu, who kept it on the Palace grounds in Saigon.

Rarity: First Class R-5; Second Class R-5

75-76 VETERANS MEDAL
Cựu-Chiến Binh Bội-Tinh
two classes — Sept. 1, 1967

Purpose: For civilians, civil servants or military personnel who accomplished meritorious service of great benefit to veterans, disabled veterans, war widows and orphans or foreigners who did meritorious service in social welfare undertakings for the benefit of the above.

Description: Front: in gold, an anchor, wings, crossed rifle and shovel, several branches of a plant, and a soldier's helmet, embellished by a green wreath, inscribed on the base of the anchor CỰU CHIẾN-BINH, 43mm. Back: plain.

75 First Class
Description: The ribbon is 10½mm, yellow 15½mm, blue 10½mm with two thread-like blue stripes 1mm apart in the center.

76 Second Class
Description: The ribbon is the same except without the two thread-like blue stripes in center.

Background: The war brought many disabled veterans, war widows, and orphans who needed help from the Veterans Ministry. A version of this medal exists with a prong back and no ribbon, perhaps for women veterans.

Rarity: First Class R-5; Second Class R-5

77-78-79 POLICE MERIT MEDAL
Cảnh-Sát Chiến-Công Bội-Tinh
three classes — Sept. 6, 1965

Purpose: For members of the National Police for distinguishing themselves by outstanding achievements such as valiantly defeating the enemy or being wounded or killed while fighting the enemy.

Description: Front: eight pointed compass rose with longer arms with balled points, surmounting a wreath, and with a central disk with a shield on a rising sun with rays and with a ribbon around inscribed at the top *TỔ-QUỐC* and, separated by two small stars on each side, at the bottom *CHI-CÔNG*, 53mm. Back: the inscription *BỘI-TINH* in a lined circle with, around, *CẢNH-SÁT* above and *CHIẾN-CÔNG* below. Suspension is by two spear points up and down crossed by a pistol and writing brush. The suspension ribbon is 45mm; green 10mm, yellow 10mm, red 5mm, yellow 10mm, green 10mm. The service bar ribbon is 37mm; green 8½mm, red 4mm, yellow 8½ mm, green 8½ mm. Sometimes this smaller ribbon was used as the suspension ribbon.

77 First Class
Description: Awarded in gold. The device on the service bar, but not used on the suspension ribbon, is a small replica of the badge in gold.
78 Second Class
Description: Awarded in silver. The device on the service bar, but not used on the suspension ribbon, is a small replica of the badge in silver.
79 Third Class
Description: Awarded in bronze. The device on the service bar, but not used on the suspension ribbon, is a small replica of the badge in bronze.
Unit Award *(Huy-Hiệu Tuyên-Công Đơn-Vị)*
Device: Ribbon in a gold frame with leaf pattern with devices as above according to class.

Background: As in many harsh civil wars, the National Police—and particularly in Vietnam, the Special Branch and the Police Field Forces—were often caught in the fighting or the operations against the Communist cadre. This medal came oddly with a specially broad 45mm ribbon.

Rarity: First Class R-5; Second Class R-5; Third Class R-4

80-81-82 POLICE HONOR MEDAL
Cảnh-Sát Danh-Dự Bội-Tinh
three classes — Sept. 6, 1965

Purpose: For members of the National Police for meritorious achievement and a period of service without blame, and for civil servants, citizens and foreigners for meritorious accomplishment in the fields of public safety and administration.

Description: Front: eight-pointed compass rose with the longer arms with balled points, surmounting a wreath, 50mm. Back: The inscription *BỘI-TINH* in a lined circle with around *CẢNH-SÁT* above and *DANH-DỰ* below. Suspension is by the police seal, consisting of a shield and book on a vertical sword surrounded with a wreath and with a ribbon below. The ribbon is green 10½mm, white 16mm, green 10½mm.

80 First Class
Purpose: For 25 years service.
Description: Awarded in gold. On the service bar, but not used on the suspension ribbon, is a device of a small gold replica of the badge.

81 Second Class
Purpose: For 20 years service.
Description: Awarded in silver. On the service bar, but not used on the suspension ribbon, is a device of a small silver replica of the badge.

82 Third Class
Purpose: For 15 years service.
Description: Awarded in bronze. On the service bar, but not used on the suspension ribbon, is a device of a small gold replica of the badge.

Unit Award *(Huy-Hiệu Tuyên-Công Đơn-Vị)*
Ribbon is in a gold frame with a leaf pattern and with devices as above according to the class.

Background: This was similar in design to the Police Merit Medal. Many police wore both unit awards.

Rarity: First Class R-5; Second Class R-5; Third Class R-4

83-84 PEOPLE'S SELF-DEFENSE MEDAL
Bội-Tinh Nhân-Dân Tự Vệ
two classes — July 7, 1969.

Purpose: For servicemen, civil servants, cadre, or other Vietnamese citizens or foreigners who distinguish themselves by meritorious service of great benefit to the organization, operation, and development of the People's Self-Defense Force, or to Vietnamese or foreign organizations, groups or associations that actively sponsor or greatly help the PSDF.

Description: Front: a Maltese cross with balled points, with small points between the rays and a large central disk with three figures in conical straw hats, one holding a rifle and another the flag of the Republic of Vietnam, with the rim inscribed above *NHÂN-DÂN TỰ-VỆ* and below with two heads of grain, 36mm. Back: in a circle a map of Vietnam with the rising sun on the left and dotted lines representing waves on the right and the inscription above *VIỆT-NAM*. The ribbon is white 4mm, blue 2½mm, red 3½mm, yellow 14mm, red 3½mm, blue 2½mm, white 4mm.

83 First Class
Description: Awarded in gold. This has a rosette on the suspension ribbon and service bar.
84 Second Class
Description: Awarded in silver. There is no rosette.

Background: The PSDF were older men and teenagers in the hamlets given US carbines and other weapons to comprise a home defense unit. While hardly able to stand up to any concerted Communist attack, they did provide some protection and psychological reassurance.

Rarity: First Class R-6; Second Class R-5

85-86 YOUTH AND SPORTS SERVICE MEDAL
Bội-Tinh Thanh-Niên Thế-Thao
two classes —Nov. 11, 1968

Purpose: For, in the field of sports, athletes who distinguish themselves by outstanding achievements in international and national competitions, by good conduct, or associations or individuals who do meritorious service to sports and physical education. In the field of youth, individuals or youth associations who do meritorious service for the Youth Service, or that have contributed to the extermination of Communism.

Description: Front: nine-sided, lightly pebbled, with red flames and with the inscription in a half circle above *THANH-NIÊN THẾ-THAO,* and below the flames the inscription *BỘI-TINH*, 36mm. Back: Inscription *VIỆT-NAM*. Suspension is by a small wreath. The ribbon is yellow 17mm, green 17mm.

85 First Class
Description: Awarded in gold. There is a rosette on the suspension ribbon and the service bar.
86 Second Class
Description: Awarded in silver. There is no rosette.

Background: The three-pointed flames pictured on this medal, signifying north, central and south Vietnam, also appear on the Vietnam Campaign medal, and, strangely also on some later Communist medals.

Rarity: First Class R-6; Second Class R-5

HAMLET COMMON DEFENSE MEDAL
Bội-Tinh Toàn-Dân Bảo-Vệ Nôn-Sông
Authorized 1963.

Purpose: For services in connection with the First Republic's National Revolution Program.

Description: Cross formee, with large central disk, bronze 39mm. Front: Cross limbs with raised borders and doubled edges beginning slightly back from the ends, with a central disk with design on right of rectangular lines indicating rice fields and on far left of city buildings, with two shocks of grain, a castle tower and a hand holding a sword with point upwards, and the inscription *NHÂN-VỊ CỘNG-ĐỒNG VÙNG-TIẾN* (Personalism, Community, Progress), with below the rim of the disk an under-rim with indented lines. Back: plain with, surmounting a circular rim, a blank bar area apparently for engraving a name. The ribbon is green 4mm, red 1mm, green 3½mm, brown 3½ mm, red 1mm, brown 2½ mm, red 1mm, brown 3½mm, green 3½mm, red 1mm, green 4mm. No ribbon bars or miniatures have been seen.

Background: It was for sale in a Saigon medal store about 1964-65. No official documentation has been seen for it, but it appears an authorized award that became obsolete with the fall of Diem and the end of the strategic hamlet program. There were a series of stamps issued in July 1963 which bore the same circular design and inscription, "Personalism, Community, Progress".

Rarity: R-9

87 PRESIDENTIAL UNIT CITATION AND STATE OF VIETNAM FRIENDSHIP RIBBON
October 7, 1954

Purpose: For United States Military Advisory Group and Naval personnel in Indochina for humanitarian services rendered during August and September 1954.

Description: No medal, only ribbon encased in gold frame. The ribbon is yellow 1/16", red 1/8", yellow 1/8", yellow 1/16", red 1/8", yellow 7/16". The Army frame is 1 3/8" by 1/2" and worn over the right pocket. The Navy and Air Force frame is 1 3/8" by 3/8" and worn in order among other ribbons over left pocket.

Background: This is also known as the Vietnam Presidential Unit Citation, and is probably worn only by American recipients. This was awarded by decree of the Vietnamese president, and approved for wear February 28, 1955. It is not known to have been awarded to Vietnamese or to other nationals.

Rarity: R-1

88 CIVIL ACTION UNIT CITATION

Purpose: For units of the ARVN, US Armed Forces and other allies in recognition of meritorious civil action service.

Description: The ribbon is dark green and red, with a narrow stripe of dark green in the center. On either side is a very thin stripe of red, a very wide dark-green stripe, a wide red stripe, and a narrow dark green stripe at the edge. The ribbon is enclosed in a gold-colored laurel leaf design with a rectangular frame.

89 GALLANTRY CROSS UNIT CITATION

Purpose: For units of the ARVN, US armed forces and other allies which distinguished themselves by gallantry in action at the risk of life. Also awarded to members of the US Armed Forces in recognition of valorous achievement in combat, March 1, 1961- March 28, 1974. Awarded for the same services that would earn the award of the Valorous Unit Citation or the Navy Unit Citation.

Description: The ribbon is red with a wide center of yellow-gold which is divided by sixteen very thin stripes of red. This large frame version is for wear by the U.S. Army.

Background: This citation was established August 15, 1950. Like the French Croix de Guerre, the Gallantry Cross used a series of emblems to designate different classes.

Army
Awarded in a bronze palm.
Corps
Awarded in a gold star palm.
Divisional
Awarded in a silver star palm.
Brigade, Regiment or similar unit
Awarded in a bronze star laurel leaf or palm.

90 GALLANTRY CROSS UNIT CITATION (NARROW)

Purpose: For members of the US Armed Forces in recognition of valorous achievement in combat, March 1, 1961—March 28, 1974. It is awarded for the same services that would earn the award of the Valorous Unit Citation or the Navy Unit Citation.

Description: The ribbon is red with a wide center of yellow gold which is divided by sixteen very thin stripes of red. This citation is a narrower version of the Gallantry Cross Unit Citation (see number 89). The ribbon is enclosed in a rectangular gold-colored frame with a laurel leaf design. Indicating this unit award was cited in Army dispatches, a small bronze laurel palm is worn on the center of the ribbon. This narrow frame version is for wear by the Navy, Marines, Air Force and Coast Guard.

91 POLICE MERIT UNIT AWARD
HUY-HIỆU TUYÊN-CÔNG ĐƠN-VỊ

Awarded to units of the National Police who had distinguished themselves against the enemy. The ribbon inside the gold-leaf frame is the same as the medal. A small replica of the medal was attached to the ribbon inside the frame.

92 POLICE HONOR UNIT CITATION
HUY-HIỆU TUYÊN-CÔNG ĐƠN-VỊ

Awarded to police units for meritorious achievement. The ribbon inside the gold frame with a leaf pattern is the same as the medal. A small replica of the medal is attached to the ribbon.

THE MEDALS OF THE ALLIES

In describing the decorations and awards of the Republic of Vietnam, it would be incomplete not to cover the medals of her allies during the Republic's battle for existence. It is useful for perspective, also, to review some of the awards of the Empire of Annam — Peaceful South, and of France for the war in Vietnam before the birth of the Republic in 1954. (The medals of the T'ai Federation and of the Nung Autonomous Zone under French sovereignty in the north of Vietnam were still worn by RVN military personnel who earned them prior to 1954.)

With almost a century of colonization, which extended from 1859 when French troops and ships participated in the expedition that seized Danang and Saigon, France influenced the design and structure of the system for the Republic's military and civilian awards. China over the centuries has had a basic impact on Vietnamese society. But in the award system, except for some scattered symbolism, only in the Kim Khanh, did the pre-French past and Chinese influence show through. On the French medals for Indochina, however, notably the modern campaign medal, there was colorful use of "oriental" design. The U.S. Vietnam Service Medal was to follow this precedent.

THE T'AI FEDERATION AND THE NUNG AUTONOMOUS ZONE

Just as all the high country of Vietnam, northwest Vietnam was the home of minority peoples. There the T'ai, distantly related to the Thai of Thailand, had a loose federation. These were the Sip Song Chau T'ai, of twelve cantons, located roughly in the vicinity of Dien Bien Phu, whose independence historically was compromised by vague pledges of loyalty to the Emperor of Annam, the King of Luang Prabang in Laos, and the Chinese Viceroy of Yunnan. Like the rest of Indochina, this area fell under French sovereignty. During the war after 1945 the French encouraged T'ai separatism as a defense against the ambitions of both the Vietnamese communists and nationalists. On March 1, 1948, the T'ai Federation was given autonomous status within the French Union with its own flag and capital at Lai Chau, and many T'ai fought with the French until the collapse after the battle at Dien Bien Phu.

The T'ai Orders of Military and Civil Merit were widely bestowed on French and Vietnamese officers, and were often seen posed to be worn in public. The decorations were manufactured both in France and in Vietnam, and were for sale in Saigon stores until the end in 1975. The inscription is in the unusual T'ai script of Nghia Lo, a variation of Sanskrit written with the Chinese brush.

Located along the northeastern border with China, the Nung Autonomous Zone, like the T'ai Federation, was also intended to be autonomous directly under the Crown of Annam, but this apparently was never formally implemented. The Nung were a minority people of mixed Muong and Hakka Chinese background, well regarded as soldiers. Some 30,000 fought on the French side, being integrated into French units as part of the "jaundicing" of the French army units during the war. After 1954, many went south, and some became the initial cadre of the ARVN 5th Division. The Nung emblems included, oddly, an umbrella handle, and also a junk inscribed on the French tricolor.

92 ORDER OF CIVIL MERIT
ORDRE DU MERITE CIVIL DES SIP HOC CHAU
four classes — 1950

Purpose: For service to the T'ai Federation by T'ai, French and others.

Description: Front: appears like four Crosses of Lorraine, the ones pointing to the top and bottom of white, and the ones pointing to the sides of black, with the longer arm overlaying the longer arm of the white crosses, and with each cross having the top and shorter arm ending in thicker squares, and with the longer arms both ending in thicker squares and having a thick square midway in the arm, and with a central square medallion with gold border inscribed in T'ai script *"Muong-Ta"* (Federation T'ai); Back: same but inscribed FEDERATION TAI. The ribbon is black 8mm, yellow 2mm, black 4mm, yellow 9mm, black 4mm, yellow 2mm, black 8mm

Grand Cross - star and cravat
Description: cravat badge is as above, 55mm. Star is in gold of eight sets of five trefoil rounded rays, surmounted with badge as above, 88mm. The sash ribbon is as above but 100mm with stripes in same proportions. The service bar ribbon has a rosette with gold wings.

Commander - cravat
Description: cravat badge is as above, 55mm. The service bar ribbon has a rosette with silver wings.

Officer - breast badge with rosette
Description: as above, 43mm. The service bar ribbon has a rosette.

Knight - breast badge
Description: as above, 43mm. The service bar ribbon is without a rosette

Background: The Vietnamese-made version is a little cruder with larger lettering.

Rarity: Grand Cross R-10; Commander R-7; Officer R-5; Knight R-4

93 ORDER OF MILITARY MERIT
ORDRE DU MERITE MILITARIES DES SIP HOC CHAU
1950

Purpose: For acts of gallantry and service to the T'ai Federation in the military field.

Description: Front: a sixteen-pointed star of silver, 48mm, with points alternately shorter and longer, and in the center a dark blue disk inscribed in T'ai script *"Muong-Ta"* (T'ai Federation), encircled with a silver beaded ring; Back: plain. Suspension is by an oval ring of darkened silver brilliants. The ribbon is black 3½mm, light blue 30mm, black 3½mm

Background: While the medal has only one class, the recipient was accorded on the award certificate a grade within the order.

Rarity: R-4

94 MEDAL OF THE NUNG AUTONOMOUS ZONE
MEDAILLE DU TERRITOIRE AUTONOME NUNG — two classes — 1954

Purpose: For military personnel and civil officials of Nung ethnic origin who served meritoriously.

Description: Round, gold 34mm. Front: stylized Chinese junk with two Chinese characters meaning "loyalty" inscribed on the hull, surrounded with the inscription *TERRITOIRE AUTONOME NUNG* at the top, and separated on each side by a star, at the bottom, *VIỆT-NAM*. Back: plain. The ribbon in green 13mm, red 12mm, green 13mm.

First Class
Description: The ribbon has a rosette on the suspension ribbon and the service bar.
Second Class
Description: The ribbon is without a rosette.

Background: Reputedly this was given by French army authorities, as they were leaving Vietnam, to personnel of the Nung forces who had served with them. It is uncertain whether a First Class of this medal was prepared.

Rarity: R-9

THE EMPIRE OF ANNAM AND DECLINE INTO A PROTECTORATE

In 1802, Vietnam was reunited under the first monarch of the Nguyen dynasty, Gia Long, who founded the Empire of Dai Nam (Great South), usually called Annam (Peaceful South). He had destroyed the Tay Son rebels with some French help. He was to be succeeded by Minh Mang in 1820, Thieu Tri in 1841, and then the pious and unfortunate Tu Duc in 1848. Tu Duc began a persecution of the Catholic missionaries, which provoked in 1857 a joint French-Spanish punitive expedition to seize Danang and Saigon. Despite heavy losses, primarily from tropical diseases, the French stayed on to keep Saigon, forcing the Court at Hue to cede the southern six provinces in 1862 and 1865 to become the French colony of Cochin China. A French naval expedition captured the citadel at Hanoi in 1873, and forced the Court to acknowledge French rights in Indochina. After French forces repulsed a Chinese intervention in Tonkin, the Court was compelled to sign a convention which effectively ended the independence of Dai Nam.

In 1887, central Vietnam (also called Annam), Tonkin, the colony of Cochin China, and Cambodia, and later the Protectorate of Laos, were brought together in an Indochina Union, usually termed French Indochina. Annam was ruled as an indirect protectorate, with the Emperor and the Court of Hue still in place, although the French resident superior had the real power. The mandarins, however, had a significant role in local administration. Tonkin was ruled as a direct protectorate with the French resident superior taking the role of the former Annamese viceroy. Although the French Government General effectively ruled Vietnam, the French authorities continued to support the largely ceremonial role of the Emperor in hope of maintaining political stability.

Despite many French contributions to modern development, the proud and nationalistic Vietnamese bridled under French colonial rule. Periodic rebellions took place, one led by the young Emperor Ham Nghi in 1884, who was soon caught, deposed and exiled. Succeeding Emperors, Dong Khanh in 1885, Thanh Thai in 1888, Duy Tan in 1907, Khai Dinh in 1916, and Bao Dai in 1925, were given respect but not authority by the French.

Bao Dai tried to press the nationalistic cause, as young Vietnamese inspired by the Chinese and Russian revolutions began to plot against French rule. In March 1945, the occupying Japanese had Bao Dai declare independence. In August 1945, in view of the ascendancy of Ho Chi Minh and the communist Democratic Republic of Vietnam, Bao Dai and his advisors decided on his abdication.

As their war against the Viet Minh grew more difficult, the French contemplated the "Bao Dai Solution", rallying non-communist Vietnamese under Bao Dai in a partially independent Vietnam tied to the French Union. In the 1949 Elysee Agreement and accords, the French agreed to a measure of independence, but not enough to accord Bao Dai the nationalist prestige he needed to rival the communists. His support fell away, and on the French collapse, a determined Ngo Dinh Diem moved to consolidate his position. A carefully arranged referendum of October 23, 1955, delivered an overwhelming vote against Bao Dai. The Republic of Vietnam was established on October 28, and Bao Dai left for the Riviera.

Background: The Court at Hue, beginning in the reign of Minh Mang, developed a system of awards adapted, like most things in Vietnam, from a Chinese model. The primary decoration was the Khanh in gold, shaped like a traditional gong, with a suitably felicitous inscription in Chinese characters, and suspended from a cord, with tassels below. The women's equivalent was the Boi. For lesser awards of merit, coin-like gold and silver pieces called Tien were presented and worn in the same way. There was also gold and ivory Bai worn on the robes that had some of the character of an award, although primarily a badge of rank and position.

The French were to initiate a number of awards for French Indochina that were the local equivalent of those of the individual ministries in France, for instance, a medal of honor for customs officials. They encouraged the Court also to develop European-style awards suspended from ribbons, and the Tiens thus were changed to that style. An Order of Agricultural Merit in three classes was also presented by the Court. But the primary decoration of the Court was the Order of the Dragon of Annam with its five classes in the fashion of the French Legion of Honor. This extensively bestowed order was the predecessor of National Order of the Republic of Vietnam, which was to keep the same ribbon. It is included here because of its historical relevance to the National Order.

95 ORDER OF THE DRAGON OF ANNAM
Đại-Nam Long-Tinh Huy-Chuong/Ordre du Dragon de l'Annam
five classes — Mar. 14, 1886

Purpose: For civil and military merit in the service of the Emperor and the Protectorate.

Description: Front: on an eight-pointed star of faceted rays, a blue oval medallion with four Chinese-style characters in seal script "Đông-Khánh Hoàng-Đế" (Emperor Đông-Khánh) in gold, with decorative lines of flame, encircled with a red riband; Back: plain. Suspension of a Western crown, with above that a green dragon facing left with, usually, red on its head. The ribbon as awarded from 1886 to 1916 for the military division was orange-yellow 7mm, white 22mm, orange-yellow 7mm. As awarded from 1886 to 1916 for the civil division it was orange-yellow 7mm, light green 22mm, orange-yellow 7mm. As awarded from 1900 by the Emperor of Annam, it was yellow 7mm, red 22mm, yellow 7mm. As awarded from 1900 by the President of France it was orange-yellow 7mm, light green 22mm, orange-yellow 7mm.

Grand Cross sash and star (termed in Vietnamese for the military division *Trác-Di Long-Tinh*, and for the civil division *Khôi-Kỳ Long-Tinh*).

Description: the sash badge as above, 75mm or 85mm, with gold rays. The star has round pointed and faceted rays, with the central medallion as above, but clutched by the claws of a green dragon with its head peering over the top of the medallion. The ribbon for the sash is 101 mm, as above in dimensions 17mm, 67mm, 17mm. The ribbon for the service bar is 36mm, with a rosette and gold wings.

Grand Officer (mil: *Thụ-Huấn Long-Tinh*; civ: *Chương-Hiên Long-Tinh*) star with at first a cravat, but later with a breast badge with rosette.

Description: A star as above with silver rays. The ribbon for the service bar has a rosette with one gold and one silver wing.

Commander (mil: *Sành-Nong Long-Tinh*; civ: *Biểu-Đức Long-Tinh*) cravat.

Description: As above with gold rays, 60mm, 75mm or other variations of size probably. The ribbon for the service bar has a rosette and silver wings.

Officer (mil: *Tương-Trung Long-Tinh*; civ: *Minh-Nghia Long-Tinh*) breast badge with rosette.

Description: as above with gold rays, 45mm, 50mm, 53mm (and other variations of size probably). The ribbon for the service bar has a rosette.

Knight (mil: *Khuyên-Công Long-Tinh*; civ: *Gia-Thiên Long-Tinh*) breast badge.

Description: as above with silver rays, 45mm, 50mm, 53mm (and other variations). The ribbon for the service bar is without a rosette.

Background: This order, also known as the Ordre du Dragon Vert, was awarded extensively over the years. There are many minor differences between the various French and Vietnamese manufacturers. For instance, on some the dragon is plumper and smaller and on other bigger faced and elongated. The star comes in various patterns of rays. Also there are some rare examples of the Bao Dai period. One numismatic catalog mistakenly described the seal script characters on the central medallion, which form a pattern of squiggly rectangular lines, as the map of the Imperial Palace!

Colonel Rullier has noted that the order was assumed on May 10, 1896, as a national order of France that could be awarded by the President on the recommendation of the Minister of Colonies. It also could continue to be awarded by the Emperor of Annam at his discretion. In order to avoid confusion as to whom had awarded this order it was decided in a decree of December 5, 1899, to come into effect on May 1, 1900, that the ribbon henceforth when awarded by the President would be green with orange-yellow edges, and when awarded by the Emperor would be white with orange-yellow edges. These ribbons had hitherto been used respectively for the civil and military classes of the Annamese awards. (The military ribbon had not been recognized by the authorities in France.) Since the white ribbon resembled that of the Royal Order of Cambodia, the Court of Hue decided to change the ribbon to one of red with yellow edges.

The Emperor, alone, had the right, according to the regulations, to wear the Knight's badge along with the Grand Cross (following the European monarchial precedent).

Rarity: Grand Cross R-8; Grand Officer R-7; Commander R-6; Officer R-4; Knight R-3

THE REPUBLIC OF FRANCE, AND THE CAMPAIGNS OF THE EXPEDITIONARY FORCES

The first French to fight in Indochina were the adventurers recruited at the end of the 18th century by Bishop Pigneau to act as advisors to Nguyen Anh's forces and later to build the great Western style citadels in Vietnam. The colonial empire of France in Indochina, resembling others elsewhere, depended on a ready colonial army partially composed of native levies with French officers. In the 1900's as more modern nationalist movements grew in Vietnam, the army and the police shared in their suppression. In 1940 the French forces in Indochina consisted of some 70,000 troops.

In September 1945, French troops under General Leclerc joined with the British and Indian soldiers of General Gracey to begin the reconquest of Saigon and the Delta. On March 6, 1946, Ho Chi Minh and Sainteny, the Commissioner of France, signed a preliminary convention whereby Vietnam was recognized as a "Free State" and Cochin China was to be re-united if the southerners agreed to it in a referendum. Relations soon disintegrated, however, and in mid-December the Viet Minh suddenly attacked the French garrisons and the First Indochina War was fully underway.

Over the next several months the Expeditionary Force, then some 67,000 French and Legionnaire troops, secured the major cities, and the Viet Minh went to the countryside. In the fall of 1950, the Viet Minh undertook a major offensive along the frontier which destroyed the French force at Cao Bang and took the towns of Lang Son and Mon Cay.

With Chinese supplies, the Viet Minh continued to attack French forces which relied on static defenses. After destruction of the French "Aeroterrestrial base" at Dien Bien Phu in 1954 the French lost heart. The political leaders in Paris accepted a way out at the Geneva Conference. In 1956 the last French troops left South Vietnam to be replaced by the Americans who were to fall unhappily into the Second Indochina War.

French medals were manufactured by the mint and by many private firms. The medals could be purchased by a recipient or by anyone, and are mostly still available from the mint and stores in France. There are many minor variations in their manufacture, and at one point reduced size medals (reduction) had a vogue. Some civil medals are engraved or even cast with the name of the recipient, but most medals do not bear the name of the person who received it. For all these reasons, plus Anglo-Saxon parochialism, French medals have not been a strong interest of collectors in Great Britain and the United States.

France was, of course, the patron of the State of Vietnam, although not an ally of the Republic after 1955. Its first medals for Indochina were the two Army and Navy versions of the Tonkin Medal given for actions in Indochina and China starting in 1883. The 20th Century French medals for the wars in Indochina, the Colonial Medal and the Indochina Medal, included many Vietnamese recipients who served in the French forces or the National Army, who for long afterwards were still wearing these medals or their ribbons. The French medals and the French system of awards also served as the model for the first Vietnamese awards, the Gallantry Cross being based on the Croix de Guerre, which in its overseas version (*Theatre d' operations exterieurs - TOE*) was widely won by French and Vietnamese combat troops before 1954. Two other French medals were distinctively given for Indochina service, the Cross for Combatant Veterans with the bar *INDOCHINE*, and the Commemorative Medal for the 1939-45 War with the bar *EXTREME ORIENT.*

96 WAR CROSS FOR OVERSEAS THEATERS OF OPERATIONS
CROIX DE GUERRE - THEATRES D'OPERATIONS EXTERIEURS
1921

Purpose: For feats of bravery or ability in war performed outside of metropolitan France.

Description: Front: A bronze straight-angled cross pattee, with crossed swords in the angles, and a central disk with the head of a woman symbolic of the Republic facing right with the inscription above *REPUBLIQUE FRANCAISE* and below two palm leaves; Back: Same design but with the central disk inscribed *THEATRES D'OPERATIONS EXTERIEURS.* The ribbon is 37mm, light blue with 9mm red edges. The devices are a bronze star for mention in brigade, regimental, or units dispatches, a silver star for mention in a divisional dispatch, a gilt star for mention in an army corps dispatch, and a bronze palm for mention in an army dispatch. A silver palm was worn instead of five bronze palms.

Background: This was based on the great French Croix de Guerre founded in 1915 for the First World War, in that case with dates on the reverse and a different ribbon. The Croix de Guerre was revived for World War II with still different dates and ribbon. This version above was distinctive to indicate combat in the colonies overseas. It was not awarded for the war in Algeria since that was part of Metropolitan France. This Croix de Guerre exists in versions with simply *T.O.E.* on the reverse, as well as slightly different arrangements of the inscription. It also exists in more recent gilt versions and deluxe versions in silver, along with crudely cast examples made in Indochina and other colonies.

Rarity: R-1

97 COLONIAL MEDAL
MEDAILLE COLONIALE
July 26, 1893
(with clasps for Indochina)

Purpose: For participation in campaigns in the French colonies and protectorate countries.

Description: Round, silver. Front: Wearing a helmet, wreath, and armor, the head of a woman symbolic of the Republic facing left with the inscription around *REPUBLIQUE FRANCAISE*. Back: In the center a globe on an anchor and trophy of arms and flags, and the inscription around the bottom *MEDAILLE COLONIALE*. Suspension is by two laurel branches. The ribbon is light blue 1½mm, white 2mm, light blue 11mm, white 7mm, light blue 11mm, white 2mm, light blue 1½mm.

The Colonial Medal as awarded for the war in Indochina 1945 to 1954 comes with the typical French bar (agrafe) inscribed *EXTREME ORIENT* (Far East). The bars are silver, 40mm by 10mm. They come in many small varieties of lettering and of edging, for instance, some are covered with edges of small straight lines. The bar *INDOCHINE* was given for operations in Indochina from 1935 to 1941. It also comes in a more elaborate "Oriental" style design usually used for the North African campaign bar. Bars for the earlier French campaigns in Indochina include *COCHINCHINE* for the operations there between 1857 and 1872, *TONKIN* for the operations there between 1893 and 1928, *HAUT MEKONG* for operations in upper Laos in 1897, *LAOS ET MEKONG* for operations in Laos and along the Mekong River between 1880 and 1909, and *ASIE* for various scientific expeditions in Indochina between 1882 and 1920. Some unofficial bars also exist, for instance, an early one *CAMBODGE* for Cambodia.

Background: The designer was G. Lemaire. The medal was 31mm and, originally, had foliage on both sides of the suspension. Circa 1920-30 medals, were to have foliage only on front of the suspension. The Colonial Medal, manufactured by both the mint and private companies, and awarded over a long period of time with many different bars, comes in many more varieties than indicated above. These include both "official" ones struck by the Mint in Paris with its mintmark and the many "unofficial" ones manufactured, as is authorized under French law, by private firms. Chobillion, for instance sold the Colonial Medal in sizes of 30mm, 25mm, 20mm, 15mm, 13mm, and 11mm. Besides size, noticeable differences include the lettering, the design of the cuirass, the lack or presence of a thin rim, and the softness of "La Republique's" features. Apparently the first ones issued in the 1890's did not have the laurel branch suspension piece. There are later examples with a fixed laurel branch suspension. The "unofficial" medals are usually smaller in size than the "official" ones.

Some of the Colonial Medals, perhaps manufactured in Indochina, are crudely made or even uniface. Ones inscribed *ETAT FRANCAIS* were manufactured in Vietnam and perhaps elsewhere during the Petain period. The early bars came with a clip on the back. Later they all had a fixed thin strip on the back to hold the bar on the ribbon. After President DeGaulle wisely dissolved the French Empire, and in the process retained strong French influence over most of the former colonies, this medal was by a decree of June 1962 replaced by the Overseas Medal. The medal remains the same except that *MEDAILLE COLONIALE* on the reverse was replaced by *MEDAILLE D'OUTREMER*. It has been given with the gilt bar *CAMBODGE* for French troops who participated in the U.S. peacekeeping missions in Cambodia. Mr. J. Hass has compiled a list of 117 different bars, official and non-official, for this medal.

Rarity: R-1, but depending on the variety.

98 INDOCHINA MEDAL
MEDAILLE COMMEMORATIVE DE LA CAMPAGNE D'INDOCHINE
Aug. 1, 1953

Purpose: For operations in Indochina with service of 90 days after Aug. 16, 1945

Description: Round, 33-35mm. Front: in the center *INDOCHINE* in a rectangular frame, below the Naga, the seven-headed cobra representing Cambodia, above the Erawan, the three-headed elephant with tiered umbrella on top representing Laos, and the inscription around the top *REPUBLIQUE FRANCAISE*. Back: in the center a wreath, half olive leaves and half oak leaves with a blank space between, and around the edge the inscription *CORPS EXPEDITIONNAIRE FRANCAISE D'EXTREME ORIENT* with a small star at the bottom. Suspension is by a coiled dragon, representing Vietnam. The ribbon is green 1½mm, yellow 4½mm, green 4½mm, yellow 4½mm, green 4½mm, yellow 4½mm, green 4½mm, yellow 4½mm, green 1½mm.

Background: The early version was in bronze while the later ones were made in gilt. An early Vietnamese-made version had the Naga reduced to more abstract design with the back inscription in three horizontal lines *CORPS EXPEDITIONNAIRE EXTREME ORIENT*. French servicemen in Indochina during this period received both the Indochina Medal and the Colonial Medal with bar *EXTREME ORIENT*. It was also awarded to all the native troops in the French units and to the servicemen of the forces of the Associated States. In the Maison Platt auction of May 26-27, 1986 two odd examples of this award were sold. They had the unofficial bar *DIEN BIEN PHU*, and had the reverse wreath shaved off and the following engraved in three lines: *A L'HONNEUR PERDU, AU COURAGE BAFOUE, A LA FIDELITE TRAHIE*. Reflecting the normal variety of local medal usage, examples of this award are known with the unofficial bars *INDOCHINE* and *ENGAGE VOLONTAIRE*, and with the red enamel wound star. The ribbon has the colors of the stripes reversed from the Tonkin Medal of the 19th Century.

Rarity: R-1 (Vietnamese made R-4).

99 MEDAL FOR THE WOUNDED
MEDAILLE DES BLESSES
1916

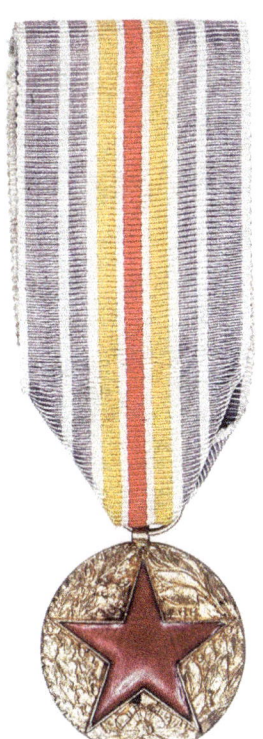

Purpose: For those wounded in combat or invalided because of illness contracted in war.

Description: Round, 32mm. Front: a red star surmounting a gilt wreath; Back: plain. The ribbon is 37mm, white 1mm, yellow 3mm, white 1mm, yellow 3mm, white 1mm, red center 3mm, white 1mm, yellow 3mm, white 1mm, blue 3mm, white 1mm, blue 5mm, white 1mm.

Background: This award officially is just a ribbon. Later medals for this came to be worn unofficially. The ones made in Vietnam are somewhat cruder. By a decree of November 8, 1952, a silver bar bearing a red star was authorized for the wounded to be worn on the appropriate campaign medal. This replaced simple red stars that were sometimes worn on the campaign medal instead of this medal. There is another version of this medal with a larger red star, on a gilt or bronze leaf-like design that curves out, but not as far as the end of the points of the star. This, of course, was not just for Indochina, but for wounded French service personnel anywhere.

Rarity: R-2

THE UNITED STATES AND A MOST COSTLY WAR

US policy towards Vietnam was to be torn between conflicting American interests in furthering nationalism, stopping the spread of communism, and avoiding entanglement on the Asian mainland. President Roosevelt felt that the French should not return to their colony at the end of World War II. The small detachment of the Office of Strategic Services that entered Vietnam in August 1945 under Colonel Patti was unsympathetic to the French efforts to regain control. Colonel Downey of that group, however, was to be the first American ground casualty in Vietnam, killed in a street ambush in Saigon. Earlier, however, planes of the 10th, 13th and 14th U.S. Army Air Forces had bombed Japanese targets in Indochina.

As the Cold War developed and as US relations with France assumed high importance in Washington, the US turned towards support for French efforts in Indochina. Spurred further by the Korean War and Chinese involvement therein, the US in 1950 began heavy military and civil aid. By 1954 the US was paying 80 percent of French military expenditures in Vietnam, some $500 million a year. The US government, however, felt the French were undercutting their effort by their refusal to give the Indochinese more independence. The French, in turn, were suspicious that the US was trying to supplant France in Indochina. As the military crisis deepened in 1954, the French requested direct US participation in the war. Some 200 US Air Force technicians were sent to help maintain the worn down French air fleet. But President Eisenhower rejected advice for intervention to save the besieged garrison at Dien Bien Phu, and the US thus did not enter the First Indochina War.

As the Diem government surprisingly seemed to succeed, the US became increasingly committed to support for the Republic of Vietnam. This was the high tide of anti-communist feeling in the US, and Diem had many American admirers. Broad civil and military aid programs were funded. The number of US military advisors and other personnel climbed from 685 in 1954 to 15,000 in 1963. The ARVN was rebuilt in the American image.

Diem's faults, however, became increasingly disturbing. Partly because he was a non-stop talker, American counsel to him was not heard, or, if heard, resented. Finally in 1963, as the restive generals plotted their coup, the US did not try to stop it. But the dismantling by the generals then of Diem's programs, and the purges of officials and offices, served further to unravel the situation in South Vietnam. The communists pressed their advantage, and President Johnson had to face the decision how much more the US should intervene militarily. For a president who remembered the Democrats labeled the "party of treason" for the "loss" of China, abandonment of South Vietnam did not see a choice. North Vietnamese attacks on an advisory compound at Pleiku and on American destroyers in the Gulf of Tonkin facilitated decisions for further US intervention. The approval on February 26, 1965, for the deployment of two US Marine infantry battalions to central Vietnam was the watershed for full involvement in the Second Indochina War.

The military buildup continued steadily to 267,000 in 1966 and to a peak strength of 543,000 US troops in early 1969, and was then to fall away equally as fast. The Marines of the 1st and 3rd Divisions were deployed in I Corps in central Vietnam. Composed together of up to eight Marine infantry regiments, they were heavier in infantry strength and lighter in weaponry than the army divisions, and also not used to digging in for protracted combat such as at Khe Sanh. With the continuous fighting and regular patrolling in mine infested populated areas they took more casualties than in the noted actions of World War II. The 1st Airmobile Cavalry Division and the 101st Airborne Division, which used helicopter tactics heavily, were moved around considerably within Vietnam. The 1st and 25th Infantry Divisions fought extensively just north of Saigon, the 4th Infantry Division mainly in central Vietnam, and the 23rd or Americal Infantry Division in I Corps. The 9th Infantry Division used one of its brigades in combination with "brown water" navy units in the mobile Riverine Force in the Delta. Independent units included the 173rd Airborne Brigade, the 11th Armored Cavalry Regiment, the 3rd Brigade of the 82nd Airborne Division, the 199th Infantry Brigade, the 1st Brigade, and others, some temporarily. The Special Forces operated along, and also surreptitiously across, the border. The Navy was heavily engaged in patrolling for blockade arms runners and in mounting the carrier operations. Both the Navy planes operating from the fleet in the Tonkin Gulf and Air Force aircraft operating from bases in Thailand in their raids on the north faced the world's most advanced and extensive anti-aircraft system.

The American ground units, with their enormous firepower, ranged widely in search of the communist forces. During the course of the war, the communist units frequently challenged the US units, particularly in defense of base areas, but generally tried to pick places and timing of their own choosing. They depended heavily thus on the use of sanctuaries in the forests and over the border in Cambodia and Laos. The Americans never lost a major battle, but the communists kept the blood flowing such that some 46,397 US personnel died during the war.

The search and destroy missions and bombing appeared to put the communists on the defensive by 1967. The pacification program pressed by the joint military-civilian CORDS organization effectively marshaled a variety of programs aimed at robbing the communists of a population base in the south. In the Tet attack of January 30, 1968, the communists achieved a psychological victory within the US, but suffered drastic losses, including the most experienced of their veteran southern units.

In 1969 President Johnson agreed to major bombing halts to encourage peace negotiations, and President Nixon in August 1969 began the drawdown of the American forces. US units participated extensively in the incursion into Cambodia in May-June 1970, but the US combat role diminished steadily. During the March 1972 communist offensive the US ground forces were down to a brigade of the 1st Airmobile Cavalry Division and had little role. US air power, however, was a critical factor in breaking the offensive. Nixon's orders in May and later in December for renewed bombing of the north and mining of ports also influenced the communists to alter their approach.

On January 27, 1973, after US coercion of a skeptical President Thieu, agreements were signed in Paris for peace in Vietnam. The accords stipulated that US and other foreign troops were to depart within 60 days, which they did, leaving only a large US military attaché staff and civilian technicians. With no trust on either side, and with Hanoi renewing its attack, the accords quickly fell apart. In sore political distress, President Nixon was unable to carry out pledges of continued support for the Republic of Vietnam, and the Congress indicated its repudiation of Vietnam by drastically curtailing aid. When the communists mounted their final 1975 offensive, US military involvement was limited to transporting the fleeing Americans and Vietnamese.

 ## 100 VIETNAM SERVICE MEDAL
July 8, 1965

Purpose: For service in Vietnam, Laos, Cambodia, contiguous waters, and in Thailand if in support of operations in Vietnam.

Description: Round bronze 1⁻". Front: dragon behind a grove of bamboo, with below inscription *REPUBLIC OF VIETNAM SERVICE*. Back: crossbow surmounted with torch, with above inscription *UNITED STATES OF AMERICA*. The ribbon is green 3/32", yellow 5/16" red 1/16", yellow 5/32", red 1/16", yellow 5/32", red 1/16", yellow 5/16", green 3/32". Devices are bronze stars, 5/32", for each campaign period and silver stars 5/32", for each five campaign periods.

Seventeen campaigns were designated:

1.	Vietnam Advisory	Mar. 15, 1962 - Mar. 07, 1965
2.	Vietnam Defense	Mar. 08, 1965 - Dec. 24, 1965
3.	Vietnam Counteroffensive	Dec. 25, 1965 - June 30, 1966
4.	Vietnam Counteroffensive Phase II	July 01, 1966 - May 31, 1967
5.	Vietnam Counteroffensive Phase II	June 01, 1967 - Jan. 29, 1968
6.	Tet Counteroffensive	Jan. 30, 1968 - Apr. 01, 1968
7.	Vietnam Counteroffensive Phase IV	Apr. 02, 1968 - June 30, 1968
8.	Vietnam Counteroffensive Phase V	July 01, 1968 - Nov. 01, 1968
9.	Vietnam Counteroffensive Phase VI	Nov. 02, 1968 - Feb. 22, 1969
10.	Tet 69 Counteroffensive	Feb. 23, 1969 - June 08, 1969
11.	Vietnam Summer-Fall	June 09, 1969 - Oct. 31, 1969
12.	Vietnam Winter-Spring	Nov. 01, 1969 - Apr. 30, 1970
13.	Sanctuary Counteroffensive	May 01, 1970 - June 30, 1970
14.	Vietnam Counteroffensive Phase VII	July 01, 1970 - June 30, 1971
15.	Consolidation I	July 01, 1971 - Nov. 30, 1971
16.	Consolidation II	Dec. 01, 1971 - Mar. 29, 1972
17.	Vietnam Cease Fire	Mar. 30, 1972 - Jan. 28, 1973

A bronze arrowhead was authorized for wear by personnel who actually participated in a landing in the vicinity of Kontum, Vietnam February 27, 1967. A bronze device of the Marine Corps symbol (globe on an anchor with eagle above) was authorized for Navy personnel attached to Fleet Marine Force units participating in combat operations.

The Vietnamese-manufactured versions of this medal are usually in gilt, and more crudely made with the usual coarse ribbon with unbound edges. The dragon is usually placed in front of the bamboo, the planchet is sometimes uniface, and the inscription on the front *VIETNAM* may be spelled *VIET NAM* or *VIET-NAM*. The Japanese-made copies are closer to the American-made ones, but differences can be seen in the dragon and the bamboo leaves.

Background: The Vietnam Service Medal carried the colors of the flag of the Republic of Vietnam, and is being worn now, long after the Republic itself has been extinguished. The colors of the ribbon on the Vietnam Service Medal were also used for the battle streamers that adorn the flags of Armed Forces units that participated in the Vietnam War. The streamers are 3 feet long and 2 ∫ inches wide. The Army and Air Force practice is to have a streamer embroidered with the name of each individual action, which for the Vietnam War would be the separate campaigns. The Navy and Marines use one streamer for each war or theater of operations, with embroidered stars for individual battles and operations deemed suitable for special recognition. The Navy battle streamer for Vietnam is embroidered, for example, with two silver and four bronze stars.

Rarity: R-1

101 CIVILIAN SERVICE IN VIETNAM AWARD Dec. 18, 1967

Purpose: For civilian employees of the US Government for an aggregate of one year's service in Vietnam after January 1, 1962.

Description: Round, bronze 1˜". Front: dragon enclosing a torch, with inscription *VIETNAM* above and *SERVICE* below. Back: US shield enclosed in two laurel branches, with inscription above *GOVERNMENT OF* and below *THE UNITED STATES*, separated by a star on either side. The ribbon is dark blue 1/8", yellow 1/16", red 1/16", yellow 1/16", dark blue 9/32", yellow 1/16", red 1/16", yellow 1/16", dark blue 1/32", yellow 1/16", red 1/16", yellow 1/16", dark blue 1/8".

Background: This civilian US Service in Vietnam Medal was originated as a morale measure for civilians who were taking their casualties also in Vietnam. The award of this was supervised by the Bureau of East Asia and Pacific Affairs in the Department of State. A recent striking has a darkish, lacquered look to it.

Rarity: Original make R-2; later make R-1

102 ARMED FORCES EXPEDITIONARY MEDAL Dec. 4, 1961

Purpose: For service in regard to US operations of assistance to friendly foreign countries.

Description: Round bronze 1˜". Front: radiant compass rose of eight points, on which is an eagle (with ribbon) with wings inverted standing upon a sword loosened in its scabbard, with inscription above *ARMED FORCES* and below *EXPEDITIONARY MEDAL*. Back: US shield, below—laurel leaves separated by dot, above—inscription *UNITED STATES OF AMERICA*. The ribbon is green 3/32", yellow 3/32", brown 3/32", black 3/32", light blue 7/32", blue 1/16", white 1/16", red 1/16", light blue 7/32", black 3/32", brown 3/32", yellow 3/32", green 3/32". Devices are bronze stars, 5/32" in size for subsequent awards.

Background: This medal was awarded for service in Laos, Apr. 19, 1961-Oct 7, 1962; Vietnam July 1, 1958-July 3, 1965; Thailand July 1, 1958-July 3, 1965; Cambodia (Evacuation - Operation Eagle Pull) April 11-13, 1975; Vietnam (Evacuation - Operation Frequent Wind) Apr. 29-30, 1975 and Mayaguez Operation May 15, 1975. When received for service in Vietnam before July 3, 1965, it may be exchanged for the Vietnam Service Medal, but the recipient may not wear both for service during that period. Rarity: R-1.

103 HUMANITARIAN SERVICE MEDAL 1974

Purpose: For meritorious participation in a significant military act or operation of a humanitarian nature performed after April 1, 1975.

Description: Round, bronze 1˜". Front: opened palm of a hand extending to upper left, surrounded by a circle. Back: oak branch of three leaves and acorns with inscription below around rim *UNITED STATES ARMED FORCES* and above *FOR HUMANITARIAN SERVICE*. The ribbon is violet 5/32", white 1/16" light blue 5/16", very dark blue 1/4", light blue 5/15", white 1/16", violet 5/32". Devices were originally bronze block numerals to indicate number of additional awards. After 1985, bronze 3/16" stars for each additional award, and silver 3/16" stars for each additional five awards were used.

Background: This medal has been awarded for many operations, including in relation to Indochina: Operation Frequent Wind (RVN); Operation Baby Lift (RVN); Operation Eagle Pull (Cambodia, Thailand); Evacuation of Laos, and Operation New Life/New Arrival (RVN, Thailand). Rarity: R-1

104 COLORADO NATIONAL GUARD ACTIVE SERVICE RIBBON (with clasp "VIETNAM CONFLICT") Sept. 11, 1963, with clasp authorized for Vietnam 1969

Purpose: For members of the Colorado National Guard who participated in active service in connection with Vietnam from Jan. 26, 1968 to Apr. 30, 1969.

Description: No medal, only service bar with clasp. Ribbon is red 3/16", yellow 1/8", white 1/8", blue 1/2", white 1/8", yellow 1/8", red 3/16". The device is bronze 3/4" x 1/8" inscribed *VIETNAM CONFLICT.*

Background: The previous Active Service Medal had been established on Apr. 14, 1931 and was replaced by the Active Service Ribbon on Sept. 11, 1963. Other states which reportedly authorized their federal active service medals for national guardsmen who served in the Vietnam War are Louisiana, Mississippi, and Texas, but there is no distinguishing mark on the awards indicating issuance was for Vietnam.
Rarity: R-3 (but seldom seen)

105 MERCHANT MARINE VIETNAM SERVICE BAR May 22, 1968

Purpose: For American merchant marine seamen who served aboard US flag vessels in Vietnam waters between July 4, 1965 and Aug. 15, 1973

Description: Round, bronze 1 5/16". Front: Anchor with superimposed disk of dragon's head with rope border, on water and tropical coast, with inscription above *VIETNAM* and below *SERVICE*. Back: Anchor on American shield with inscription above *UNITED STATES* and below *MERCHANT MARINE*. The ribbon is dark blue 1/8", yellow 13/32", red 1/16", yellow 1/6" red 1/16", yellow 1/16" red 1/16", yellow 13/32", dark blue 1/8".

Background: This originally was just a ribbon bar like the other American Merchant Marine campaign awards. It was authorized by Public Law 822 of the 89th Congress. Under a Congressional Act of 1988, after many pleas by merchant mariners, medals for these campaign awards were authorized and designed. Rarity: R-1

106 COMMEMORATIVE MEDAL FOR FAMILIES OF AMERICAN PERSONNEL MISSING IN SOUTHEAST ASIA Sept. 1983

Purpose: For the next of kin of Americans, military and civilian, listed as missing in Southeast Asia.

Description: Round, bronze 3". Front: Eagle perched in a bamboo grove with the inscription around *MISSING WHILE SERVING IN THE DEFENSE OF FREEDOM IN SOUTHEAST ASIA*, separated by two stars from the inscription below *POW* (star) *MIA.* Back: Image of the regular Vietnam Service Medal with the inscription above *YOU ARE NOT FORGOTTEN* and below *BY ACT OF CONGRESS SEPTEMBER 1983*, and around *HONORING AMERICANS STILL MISSING* separated by four stars from inscription below 1961 (star) *VIET-NAM* (star) *LAOS* (star) *CAMBODIA* (star) 1973. The ribbon is a cravat, of the same ribbon for the Vietnam Service Medal.

Background: This was approved as an amendment to the Department of Defense Authorization Act of 1984 for the 2,494 families of the missing. A 1-5/16" version without ribbon is sold by the U. S. Mint. Rarity: presentation medal R-10; mint copy R-1

THE COMMONWEALTH AND SOME HELP FOR FRIENDS

Under the Potsdam Agreements, the British were to take the Japanese surrender in the southern half of Indochina while the Chinese took it in the north. General DeGaulle—suspicious of his allies' intentions and anxious to preserve France's position in Indochina—had established the French Expeditionary Forces of the Far East within General Mountbatten's Southeast Asia Command. General Leclerc and Admiral Thierry d'Argenlieu were appointed respectively Commander-in-Chief and High Commissioner for Indochina. General Gracey was selected to lead the British force to enter south Vietnam, and was instructed to disarm the Japanese and not become involved in maintaining order.

General Gracey and the first elements of his 20th Indian Division arrived in Saigon September 12-13, 1945, to find a highly confused situation as Vietnamese Communists and nationalists were trying to establish independence, the bitter French were attempting to restore their authority, and the defeated Japanese forces were being called on to help maintain order. Blood was being spilled as first the Vietnamese and then the French took provocative action against the other. General Gracey banned demonstrations and took measures to curb the Viet Minh's Committee of the South. In hazard of his instructions, Gracey effectively allied his forces with the French under Leclerc, and substantially aided thus the French reconquest by the end of the year. The division consisted of the 80th (the first to arrive), 32nd, and 100th Indian Infantry Brigades. The 16th Light Calvary Squadron and Spitfire Squadron 1273 also participated in the action against the Viet Minh, which cost the British forces 23 dead. On January 1, 1946, the British ships departed Saigon, and General Gracey followed at the end of the month. The Southeast Asian Command relinquished authority south of the 16th parallel to General Leclerc on March 4.

The next Commonwealth troops in South Vietnam were a party of 30 Australian Army military instructors who arrived in June 1962 to assist the ARVN in central Vietnam. The Australian Army Training Team in Vietnam grew by 1965 to a complement of some 200, all officers and warrant officers. An aviation unit of some 74 men and six Caribou cargo aircraft also was in Vietnam in 1964.

Although the American debate over Vietnam was fiercely echoed in Australia, the government of Prime Minister Menzies strongly supported the US effort. In response to President Johnson's request, Menzies announced that: "I have assured him of Australia's continuing assistance in the defense of South Vietnam." The 1st Battalion, The Royal Australian Regiment, arrived in Vietnam in May and June 1965. The size of the Australian Army Force, Vietnam, steadily increased to some 7,600 men in three maneuver battalions, plus a naval contingent (first the H.M.A.S. Hobart, a guided missile destroyer) and helicopter and fixed air wings units. The Australians' Task Force proved to be some of the best troops in Vietnam and had the most commendable record of the allied participation.

In line with the ANZAC tradition, New Zealand also supplied a New Zealand Force, Vietnam, which grew to some 550 men, primarily artillery with support infantry and logistic units. These were integrated with the Australian units and performed equally well.

108 CAMPAIGN SERVICE MEDAL (1962) Oct. 6, 1964, with clasp for South Vietnam authorized June 8, 1968

Purpose: For officers and warrant officers of the Australian Army Training Team who served thirty days in South Vietnam between Dec. 24, 1962, and May 28, 1964.

Description: Round, silver, 36mm. Front: crowned head of Queen Elizabeth II, with inscription *ELIZABETH II DEI GRATIA REGINA F. D.* Back: round oak wreath with inscription inside *FOR CAMPAIGN SERVICE,* surmounted with crown; ornamental suspension bar. The ribbon is green 5mm, violet 22mm, green 5mm. The bar is plain silver 4mm in height inscribed *SOUTH VIETNAM.*

Background: The CSM exists with many other clasps for United Kingdom and Commonwealth military involvements, but it is very rare, with this clasp, since only 68 Australian officers and warrant officers qualified for it. The Australian Vietnam Service Medal was awarded for service after May 28, 1964. The earlier General Service Medal and Naval General Service Medal have the clasp *S.E. ASIA 1945-46* for the British and Indian forces who served in Indochina and Indonesia to maintain order after World War II. The official title for this medal is "General Service Medal." Rarity: R-10 (Authentically engraved with recipient's name)

109 AUSTRALIAN AND NEW ZEALAND SERVICE MEDAL VIETNAM
June 28, 1968

Purpose: For operational service in Vietnam for thirty days after May 29, 1964.

Description: Round silver 36mm. Front: crowned head of Queen Elizabeth II, with inscription *ELIZABETH II DEI GRATIA REGINA F.D.* Back: nude male figure between two spheres with inscription above *VIET-NAM*. It is suspended by an ornamental bar. The ribbon is light blue 5mm, red 3mm, yellow 5mm, red 1mm, yellow °mm, red 1mm, yellow °mm red 1mm, yellow 5mm, red 3mm, dark blue 5mm. The ribbon may also bear the oak leaf device, if the recipient was awarded it for Mention in Dispatches.

Background: The well-known British and Commonwealth system of awards was also enriched by the Vietnam War. The Australians and New Zealanders earned many decorations, not only from the British system (including four Victoria Crosses) but from the US and Republic of Vietnam also. A draft Royal Warrant to allow the wearing of the latter decorations was not approved, so those many awards are not worn in uniform by the Australian servicemen. The exceptions are the Vietnamese Campaign Medal (named on the back) and apparently, also, the Life Saving Medal. The Australians and New Zealanders who received the American unit awards usually wear them in their frames on the upper sleeves of the uniform.

Rarity: R-4

110 VIETNAM LOGISTICS AND SUPPORT MEDAL
Aug. 23, 1992

Purpose: For Austrialian military and naval personnel who supported the operations in Vietnam between May 19, 1964, and Jan. 27, 1973.

Description: Round, silver, 36mm - Obv: crowned head of Queen Elizabeth II with inscription *ELIZABETH II DEI GRATIA REGINA F.D.*; Back: nude male figure between two spheres with inscription about *VIET-NAM*. It is suspended by a plain straight bar. The ribbon is 4mm, dark blue 3mm, yellow 7mm, red 1mm, yellow 1mm, red 1mm, yellow 1mm, red 1mm, yellow 7mm, dark blue 3mm, light blue 3mm.

Background: The late issue of this medal was in response to the pleas of those who supported the forces in Vietnam but who were excluded from receipt of the first award by the strict terms of entitlement. Stocks of the original planchets in real silver of the Australian and New Zealand Service Medal will reportedly be used until exhausted, and then new planchets will be manufactured in composition metal. The suspension for this medal is different from the original one, being plain and straight.

Rarity: R-6

THE REPUBLIC OF KOREA
AND THE CAUSE OF ANOTHER DIVIDED NATION

Positioned at either end of China's littoral, Korea and Vietnam had resembled each other as heavily Chinese influenced tributary states. In our times they both were to suffer division into communist and non-communist halves.

As early as 1954, President Rhee had offered, without response, to send troops to assist in Vietnam against the Communists. In 1964, the Republic of Korea offered and sent to Vietnam a Mobile Army Surgical Hospital (MASH) and ten Taekwondo instructors. This was followed in early 1965 by a contingent of ROK Army and Marine engineers, a security company, and some LSM's and LST's, all designated the ROK Military Assistance Group and nicknamed the Dove Unit.

President Park, during his visit to Washington in May 1965, agreed to furnish also a combat infantry division of some 18,212 men. The Korean force consisted of the Capital (Tiger) Division minus one regiment and the 2nd Marine Corps Brigade (Blue Dragon), and arrived September-November 1965. The Capital Division was positioned near Qui Nhon and the Marines further north near Tuy Hoa. The Korean Government extracted a heavy price from the US for the dispatch of the division, which included payment for the troops in Vietnam, major new equipment for and expansion of the ROK forces at home, and a program of procurement of supplies in Korea. Just as Japan profited from the Korean War, South Korea was to profit from the Vietnam War.

In the Autumn of 1966, the 9th Infantry Division (White Horse) also arrived and was stationed south of the Capital Division along the coast of central II Corps. At the peak, Korean troops totaled some 50,000 with the Corps command at Nha Trang. The Koreans agreed to operate de facto under MACV, but preserved a titular independence.

Koreans have the reputation of being tough (as well as quarrelsome), and the ROK soldiers and marines, especially those of the first tranche of volunteers, proved excellent soldiers. The Korean units planned operations methodically and carried them out meticulously, being especially proficient at combing target areas and finding many more enemy weapons than US units would in comparable operations. The major mission was area and highway security, and the ROK units were key to reversing the communist inroads in coastal II Corps. As the war went on, however, the Blue House in Seoul apparently ordered that the ROK units should minimize casualties, and the ROK units became more passive, sitting in their hilltop barbed wire forts. A running problem also was the lack of rapport between the South Koreans and the South Vietnamese, despite being fellow Asians. Beginning in December 1970 the Korean forces withdrew in concert with the US units.

From their combat operations in Vietnam, however, there was no question that the ROK army and its officer corps had made impressive professional progress since the Korean War. Vietnam was to prove useful for them as an additional combat training ground and as a lesson of the penalties of failure in a divided country.

111 VIETNAM PARTICIPATION MEDAL
WELNAM CHAMCEN KICANG

Purpose: For servicemen who served in Vietnam.

Description: Round, darkened bronze, 31mm. Front: Dove with wings spread on map of East Asia and surmounting eight thin rays, with a pebbled border. Back: In the center Armed Forces symbol of ying-yang double comma device on a five petaled flower, with inscription above in-hangul "Welnam Chamcen Kicang" (Vietnam Participation Badge), and below, between two palm branches, the inscription in hangul "Tayhan Minkwuk." (Republic of Korea). The ribbon is white 2°mm, purple 8°mm, white 2mm, purple 3mm, white 2mm, purple 3mm, white 2mm, purple 8°mm, white 2°mm.

Background: The Republic of Korea has a full system of civil and military decorations and medals which underwent major changes in organization and in design about 1951, 1967 and 1973. Now most decorations, such as the Order of Military Merit (Mugong Hujang), have been standardized at five classes plus a medal. ROK decorations were extensively presented to senior Vietnamese and US officers who worked with the Koreans. In turn, the Koreans received many US and Vietnamese decorations, and like the other Allied forces, the Korean participants in the Vietnam War earned the Vietnamese Campaign Medal. Ribbons are made up in an embroidered form, and as is US practice, are not worn on the field uniforms. The Korean-manufactured RVN Campaign Medal has American-style bound edge ribbon, but the gold points of the star badge have curved instead of straight lines. Rarity: R-4

THE KINGDOM OF THAILAND AND A TRADITIONAL RIVALRY

The Thai also were drawn into conflict as American involvement in Vietnam deepened, and as the Thai People's Liberation Army of the Communist Party of Thailand increased it's insurgent activity in the north and northeast. The US-gained major facilities and airbases in Thailand, such as Udorn and Utapao, which were used extensively for strikes on Vietnam. The Thai also quietly organized voluntary, or perhaps more accurately mercenary, infantry and artillery units under Royal Thai Army officers and NCO's for deployment in Laos to stiffen the flabby Royal Lao Army. They had in 1971 both a notable victory at Ban Houei Sai near Paksong and a defeat on the Plain of Jars, and saw considerable combat. Within Thailand the Communist Suppression Operations Command mounted a variety of counterinsurgency programs and operations of mixed effectiveness against the Communist insurgents. These guerrilla forces received most of their military training and supplies through Laos from the North Vietnamese and Chinese.

The small Thai Air Force contingent, which had been there since 1964, became a part of the Royal Thai Military Assistance Group, which was activated in Vietnam on February 17, 1966. The Air Force personnel manned some C-123's and C-47's, and the Thai Navy assisted with three landing craft in Vietnam. The first substantial ground force was the Royal Thai Army Volunteer Regiment, the Queen's Cobras, which closed in Vietnam from July to November 1967. This was a force drawn from volunteers from existing units. In 1968, after extensive consultations between the governments, a division was organized as a new, additional unit for the Thai Army to replace the regiment in Vietnam. This Royal Thai Army expeditionary division — the Black Panthers of two brigades of three maneuver battalions each — made a total Thai force of some 11,568. The Thais were stationed east of Saigon in Bien Hoa, a quiet area. The division was notable for its inactivity, but did fight well on the few occasions when it was attacked. As the US began to withdraw, so did the Thai, and the withdrawal was almost complete by April 1972.

112 VIETNAM COMBAT SERVICE MEDAL
LIEN CHAI SMORABHUM VIETNAM

Purpose: For service in Vietnam.

Description: Round, white metal 38mm. Front: war elephant and three riders in ancient combat scene, with inscription in Thai above and below. Back: in the center the inscription in the Thai language *"We fight for Thailand's Honor"* with design around the edge of the Royal discus. Suspension is by a leaf-like Thai design. The ribbon has some variation in size and shade of color; 32mm — red 4mm, white 4mm, light brown 15mm, white 4mm, red 4mm. The bar is a bronze war mace, with at one end a crown and the three headed elephant and with an inscription. The device is exploding lightning on a small gold bar, 23mm used on the suspension ribbon and the service bar, designating combat service.

Background: The Thai gave separate medals to those who actually fought and those who only participated in the short 1941 war with French Indochina. The same war medal was awarded in different metals and with different ribbons for all the modern conflicts Thailand has been in, including the Vietnam war. Thai service personnel sometimes wear, instead of the full set of ribbons, just one ribbon that they consider among the more significant of their awards. This is worn like the German schnalle, in a gold (or for other awards, silver) frame like that of the US unit awards, approximately 37mm by 16mm with a leaf pattern. This is worn with the ribbon extending above and below the frame.

Rarity: R-3

83

THE REPUBLIC OF THE PHILIPPINES AND SEATO BROTHERHOOD

In August 1964, sixteen Philippine officers were sent to Vietnam as a part of the Free World Assistance Program to act as psychological warfare advisors in III Corps. In the fall of 1966 President Macapagal visited the US to meet with President Johnson and discuss a larger Filipino contribution. By doing this, the Philippine Government hoped to secure more substantial military aid from the US in part to meet a perceived threat from Indonesia. The commitment to Vietnam, however, became a contentious matter within the lively politics of the Philippines, and the final decision was to dispatch a force with only a defensive civic action mission.

The Philippine Civic Action Group, Republic of Vietnam, consisted of about 2,000 personnel, mainly an engineer battalion and a guard infantry battalion. In part as a political gesture by the Saigon government to the Cao Dai sect, the Group was stationed in Tay Ninh province. Besides its fine medical work it was primarily engaged in construction of its own base camp and of a new model community southeast of Tay Ninh city. It had the reputation of doing only a passable job of construction, defending only itself, and engaging in extensive womanizing. The US paid the costs and gave supplemental assistance to the Philippine Armed Forces. As the politics of the issue heated up in the Philippine Congress, President Marcos decided in June 1969 to withdraw the group. This was completed in February 1970. A Philippine Contingent of medical personnel remained to a later date. Many Filipino civilians did excellent work assisting in the advisory effort in the field in Vietnam.

113 REPUBLIC OF VIETNAM SERVICE MEDAL
Apr. 28, 1969

Purpose: For Armed Forces of the Philippines personnel, mainly of the Philippine Civic Action Group, in Vietnam for six months service in Vietnam from July 1954 thereafter.

Description: Round, gold bronze 38mm. Front: Dragon facing right against a partially cut bamboo grove with the inscription below *REPUBLIC OF VIETNAM SERVICE*. Back: Philippine national arms in the center, inscribed around *REPUBLIC OF THE PHILIPPINES*. The ribbon is yellow 5mm, red 4mm, yellow 4mm, blue center 10mm, yellow 4mm, red 4mm, yellow 5mm.

Background: The Philippine system of decorations and medals is closely based on the American system with many of the senior American decorations having an exact Philippine counterpart. The medals are only occasionally worn on dress uniforms. The ribbons also are not extensively worn. Exceptions are the two framed unit presidential citation ribbons, which are worn on ordinary uniform by officers and enlisted men over the right pocket. Ribbons are often in the form of enameled metal bars.

The Philippine Vietnam Service Medal is a handsomely made piece of more size and detail then the US one, although the front is similar. The maker was the official manufacturer of most Philippine medals, El Oro Engraver Corporation of Quezon City.

The regulation specifies that three silver stars should be placed in a triangle shape on the center blue ribbon but this does not seem to apply in practice. This award was authorized by the Armed Forces of the Philippines Regulation G 131-052 of April 24, 1967, as amended on April 28, 1969.

Rarity: R-4

THE REPUBLIC OF CHINA
AND ANTI-COLONIALIST, ANTI-COMMUNIST SYMPATHY

In 1954, as the US sought international support for the Republic of Vietnam, the American commanders, particularly General Walt of the Marines, were strongly interested in troops from the Republic of China. President Chiang Kai-shek on his part expressed enthusiasm for the use of his forces against North Vietnam, hopefully for experience for an eventual counterattack against the mainland. But South Vietnamese officials feared that their presence might incite traditional anti-Chinese feelings among the people, and Washington decided that the use of the Republic of China Army would alarm others whose support was needed and perhaps provoke the People's Republic of China to enter the war more actively.

The Republic of China Military Advisory Group, Vietnam, that arrived on October 8, 1964, was only some 30 officers and men who acted as political warfare advisors in Saigon and at the corps level. Taipei, however, also extended a variety of civil aid, including some landing ships.

114 MEMORIAL MEDAL OF HONOR OF THE REPUBLIC OF CHINA MILITARY ASSISTANCE GROUP TO THE REPUBLIC OF VIETNAM
CHUNG-HUA MIN-KUO ZHU-YUEH JUN-YUAN-TUAN JUNG-YU CHI-NIAN-ZHANG
c. 1968

Purpose: For personnel of the Military Assistance Group and others who cooperated with the Republic of China Military Assistance Group.

Description: A large-rayed medal, 58mm. Front: large central disk of green with R.O.C. Armed Forces device of wings, crossed sword and rifle and an anchor with the twelve-rayed white sun on a blue disk in the center, and in a semi-circle above successively red, white, blue, blue, white, red lines and below in gold two palm branches, on a star of twelve three-pointed rays, with short pointed rays between gold, with red lines engraved thereon. Back: plain. The ribbon is yellow 3° mm, red 1°mm, yellow 3mm, red 1°mm, yellow 3mm, red 1°mm, yellow 3mm, red 6mm, white 6mm, blue 6mm (sometimes reversed). Device on the ribbon is the R.O.C. national twelve-rayed sun or star.

Background: The Republic of China has a full and rather elaborate system of orders and medals, worn by their military and civil personnel in a standard manner. The government has also been lavish in its presentation of awards to foreign officers and officials, including Vietnamese senior officers. The Memorial Medal of Honor appears to have been an award made locally in Saigon for presentation by the Military Advisory Group to its personnel and those it worked with. The medal has a Chinese cast to it, is unusually large, and is made in a fashion that resembles the "beer-can distinctive insignia." It was reportedly made, however, by Phuoc Hung, a major manufacturer and seller of medals and insignia in Saigon. Rarity. R-9

THE INTERNATIONAL COMMISSIONS AND FUTILE POLICE DUTIES

The two International Commissions for Indochina were the product of the two major peace agreements and the distrust that accompanied them. The signatories required an international force to police the execution of the agreements, but in both cases the only force that could be agreed upon had to be balanced between the two sides, and was thus effectively paralyzed. The commissions were not under the auspices of the United Nations. They were arranged between the signatory parties and the governments that supplied the officials and troops of the delegations.

The first of them was the International Commission for Supervision and Control as decided on in the Geneva Conference Declaration of July 20, 1954. Under Chapter 6 of the Cessation of Hostilities, a Joint Commission of representatives of the commanders of the two sides administered the cease fire, with the International Commission responsible for overseeing proper execution by the parties. The busiest time was the first 300 days as some 80,000 Viet Minh "relocated" to the north and some 190,000 French and Vietnamese troops and well over a million refugees moved to the south. The last substantive reports of the Commission were in 1965.

The second Commission was called the International Commission of Control and Supervision, a result of the Vietnam peace agreement initialed in Paris January 24, 1973. Under Article 18 of the Cease Fire Agreement, a four member Joint Military Commission of the signatories was to conduct preliminary investigations of charges of violations of the accord, and send any disagreements to the Commission. With a total civil and military complement of 1,160 personnel, the four initial delegations of the Commission were from Hungary, Poland, Indonesia, and a reluctant Canada. But on May 29, 1973, Canadian Secretary of State for External Affairs Sharp announced the withdrawal of the Canadian contingent. They were replaced by an Iranian delegation that arrived August 30. Again the communist delegations made little effort to hide their task of defending the interests of the North Vietnamese. By April 1975, the South Vietnamese government claimed some 84,063 violations of the cease-fire with 164,383 deaths, few of which were ever investigated.

115 INTERNATIONAL COMMISSION FOR SUPERVISION AND CONTROL MEDAL 1967

Purpose: For personnel of the Commission for a 90-day tour of duty in Vietnam Indochina after August 7, 1954.

Description: Round, blackened bronze, 35mm. Front: crossed flags of Canada and Poland with above the Indian symbol of the three lions of the Asoka Pillar, with a flying dove in the center, and the inscription around the sides *INTERNATIONAL COMMISSION FOR SUPERVISION AND CONTROL,* and below *PEACE.* Back: map of Indochina, with the names of the countries written in native script. There is a fixed suspension of a straight patterned bar. The ribbon is green 10mm, white 10°mm, red brown 10mm.

Background: The green in the ribbon represents India, the red Canada and Poland, and white the peace. According to the Canadian order in regard to the medal (CFAO 18-8), the recipient's rank, surname and initials were to be engraved around the edge of the medal. This was reportedly manufactured in Bangalore, India, and has been copied in gilt in Canada.

The style of the medal — with straight suspension and English inscriptions — is vaguely British. In 1971 the Canadian government arranged for its own purchase of the medals for the Canadian members of the International Commission for Supervision and Control since the Commission apparently had no supply of its own. 1,403 Canadians were issued the first ICSC Service Medal by the Canadian Government.

Rarity: R-6

116 INTERNATIONAL COMMISSION OF CONTROL AND SUPERVISION MEDAL
March 13, 1973

Purpose: For personnel of the commission for a 90-day tour in Vietnam.

First Version
Description: Round, gold, 35mm. Front: symbols for the four participating countries going from upper left, clockwise, Canadian Maple Leaf, Hungarian Coat of Arms, Indonesian Garuda, and Polish Eagle, with the inscription *INTERNATIONAL COMMISSION OF CONTROL AND SUPERVISION* around the outside. Back: inscription *SERVICE VIETNAM 27-1-1973* bracketed by two sprays of laurel leaves. There is a linked suspension to a straight bar. The ribbon is 37mm, red 4mm, white 4mm, red 4mm, white 4mm, green 4mm, white 4mm, red 4mm, white 4mm, red 4mm.

Background: There are three varieties of this first version, respectively with a raised small maple leaf between the tips at the top of the back, with an incused maple leaf, and with no maple leaf. The first two varieties were clearly manufactured just for the Canadian contingent with the Commission.

Second Version
Description: Round, gold, 35mm. Front: symbols for the four participating countries going from upper left, clockwise, Hungarian Coat of Arms, Indonesian Garuda, Iranian Lion with Sun and Crown, Polish Eagle, with the inscription *INTERNATIONAL COMMISSION OF CONTROL AND SUPERVISION* in taller letters around the outside; Back: inscription *SERVICE VIETNAM 27 - 1 - 1973* in squatter letters bracketed by two sprays of laurel leaves. There is a linked suspension to a straight bar. The ribbon is 37mm, red 3˚mm, white 3˚mm, green 3˚mm, red 3˚mm, white 3˚mm, green 3˚mm, white 3˚mm, red 3˚mm, white 3˚mm, red 3˚mm

Background: The ICCS memorandum of March 1973, signed by Major General Ferenc Szucs, the Chairman of the Military Committee, notes that the Canadian Delegation would have the medal struck on the basis of the agreed design. Each delegation was to seek its own government's approval for its award. Some 355 Canadians were issued the second ICCS Service Medal. The colors of the ribbon represent the participating countries, with white representing peace. The suspension piece is identical to that of the Republic of Vietnam Rural Revolutionary Development Medal, undoubtedly thus indicating the same original maker.

Rarity: 1st Version R-5; 2nd Version R-7

THE FEDERAL REPUBLIC OF GERMANY AND THE KNIGHTS OF MALTA

Founded with a hospital in Jerusalem during the crusades, it was natural for the Order of Malta to provide succour for the wounded and ill in Vietnam. The Sovereign Military Order of the Hospital of St. John of Jerusalem, of Rhodes, and of Malta is a Catholic organization which enjoys extraterritoriality in Rome, although there are non-Catholic organizations of the same heritage in Great Britain and elsewhere. The Malteser Aid Service in the Federal Republic of Germany staffed the hospital ship S.S. Helgoland and a German-built hospital in Danang, part of the substantial civil aid from Germany during the war.

Earlier the Malteser Aid Service had bestowed a medal on those who had assisted in the flow of refugees from Hungary. The Order of the Malta Medal for Help for Vietnam (Erinnerungsmedaille "Hilfseinsatz Vietnam") of 1967, closely resembling the medal for aid during the Hungarian uprising, was given to doctors, nurses, and others who served in Vietnam.

ORDER OF MALTA MEDAL FOR HELP FOR VIETNAM (ERINNERUNGSMEDAILLE "HILFSEINSATZ VIETNAM") 1967

Purpose: For personnel dispatched by the Order of Malta to provide medical and other assistance in Vietnam.

Description: Round, silver 35mm, Front: shield of Maltese cross surmounted by field with initials *MHD* (Malteser-Hilfsdienst), and by another field above divided in three sections, the left and right ones appearing to be the German tricolor flags and the one in the center with the inscription *DUC* (Vietnamese for "German") and around the inscription *AVXILIVM. MELITENSE.IN.VIETNAM* and below, separated by small Maltese cross, *MCMLXVI*; Back: scene of uniformed Order of Malta men and nurses before an ambulance marked with the Maltese cross helping a prostrate figure. The ribbon is red 1mm, white 3mm, red 4mm, white 3mm, yellow 4 1/2mm, red 1mm, yellow 1/2mm, red 1mm, yellow 1/2mm, red 1mm, yellow 4 1/2mm, white 3mm, red 4mm, white 3mm, red 1mm (with buckle at top in Spanish style).

ADDENDUM

MEMORANDUM

REPUBLIC OF VIETNAM
MINISTRY OF DEFENSE
JOINT GENERAL STAFF
REPUBLIC OF VIETNAM ARMED FORCES
AWARDS & DECORATIONS DIVISION

No. 910/TTM/VP/PCP/3

SUBJECT: Awarding New Medals.

REFERENCE: Decree #205-CT/LDQG/SL, dated 2 December 1965, prescribing the authority to award medals.

I. Recently the Joint General Staff has received a number of documents recommending the award of new medals. The reasons indicated for recommendation are usually not concordant with award principles, and basic documents have been interpreted according to conflicting concepts, thus making consideration and final decisions complicated and slow.

II. The purpose of this Memorandum is to instruct agencies about the recommendation procedures for the awarding of the following distinguished medals:

    1. Army Distinguished Service Order
    2. Air Force Distinguished Service Order
    3. Navy Distinguished Service Order
    4. Army Meritorious Service Medal
    5. Air Force Meritorious Service Medal
    6. Navy Meritorious Service Medal
    7. Staff Service Honor Medal
    8. Technical Service Honor Medal
    9. Training Service Honor Medal
    10. Armed Forces Honor Medal
    11. Special Service Medal
    12. Hazardous Service Medal
    13. Air Gallantry Medal
    14. Navy Gallantry Medal
    15. Life Saving Medal

At the same time, this Memorandum prescribes the condition and procedures for awarding the above medals as applied to foreign personnel.

III. The conditions, authority and procedures for awarding the above medals are prescribed in the attached annexes (from annex 1 to 5).

IV. Agencies are to note the following items:

QUÂN KỲ QLVNCH QUÂN CHỦNG

    a) Foreign military personnel are recommended for medal awards in accordance with the same standards prescribed for Vietnamese military personnel. Addressees are reminded that there are many distinguished medals for which a Vietnamese serviceman cannot be recommended unless he has served at least one full year. The National Order of Vietnam Military Merit Medal, Army Distinguished Service Order, etcetera, are the most distinguished medals of our country and a person who receives one of these awards must have accumulated a considerable length of service and have accomplished outstanding achievements. Therefore, foreign military personnel who have served a normal tour of duty that does not exceed one year, can only be recommended for either the Armed Forces Honor Medal, the Staff Service Honor Medal, the Training Service Honor Medal, or the Technical Service Honor Medal.

    However, General Officers and Senior Advisory Officers to major units or other important agencies can be recommended for either the Army Distinguished Service Order, Air Force Distinguished Service Order, or the Navy Distinguished Service Order, if it is evident that the individuals concerned made maximum use of their ability and knowledge to fulfill many special and important projects for the Republic of Vietnam Armed Forces.

    b) Vietnamese or foreign military personnel cannot be recommended, for several different medals while serving in an assigned position even though, in that position, they achieved excellent successes in many different fields (staff, technical, training, etcetera).

Recommending officials must carefully evaluate the merits of each individual and only recommend this individual for that medal which best suits the primary function of the individual's position. This rule does not apply to the recommendation for medals awarded for courageous acts (such as the Gallantry Cross, Air Gallantry Medal, Navy Gallantry Medal, Hazardous Service Medal, and the Life Saving Medal). These medals are only respectively awarded for courageous acts. However, servicemen cannot be awarded two or more different medals for the same courageous act.

c) Addressees should not accept the erroneous proposition that a foreign serviceman serving with a combat unit can only be recommended for a medal prescribed for courageous acts such as the Gallantry Cross, Air Gallantry Medal, etcetera. Recommending officials must distinguish between deeds that are performed as a part of a man's daily task and other special acts on the battlefield. Each of these different achievements is entitled to an award with a corresponding medal. Therefore, addressees should not automatically consider the above two categories of achievement as only one when recommending awards and medals. There can be many servicemen who exhibit courage on the battlefield and be awarded the Gallantry Cross, Air Gallantry Medal, Navy Gallantry Medal or National Order of Vietnam, etc. ..., while in his primary (daily) function he has not achieved any success that is worthy of recommendation for a medal that corresponds to accomplishments in his profession, such as the Staff Service Honor Medal, Technical Service Honor Medal, etcetera. On the other hand, there are many other individuals who perform courageous acts on the battlefield that parallel outstanding accomplishments in their daily function. In this case, they can be recommended for two different types of medals during one tour of duty in Vietnam.

d) Concerning accomplishments achieved in primary functions, foreign military personnel can be recommended for one of the following types of medals, depending on the importance of their accomplishment and their position.

- National Order of Vietnam
- Army Distinguished Service Order
- Air Force Distinguished Service Order
- Navy Distinguished Service Order
- Armed Forces Honor Medal
- Staff Service Honor Medal
- Technical Service Honor Medal
- Training Service Honor Medal

e) Concerning courageous acts, personnel can be recommended for one of the following types of medals depending on the degree of courage in action, the extent of danger, and the nature of the mission completed:

- National Order of Vietnam to include the Gallantry Cross with Palm,
- Military Merit Medal to include the Gallantry Cross with Palm,
- Army Distinguished Service Order*
- Air Force Distinguished Service Order*
- Navy Distinguished Service Order*
- Army Meritorious Service Medal*
- Air Force Meritorious Service Medal*
- Navy Meritorious Service Medal*
- Special Service Medal
- Gallantry Cross
- Air Gallantry Medal
- Navy Gallantry Medal
- Hazardous Service Medal
- Life Saving Medal

*The Joint General Staff is currently considering placing an additional special marking on the ribbons of these 6 medals in order to distinguish these awards between those given for courageous acts and those awarded for primary functions.

Recommendations for the awarding of medal to acknowledge courageous acts are never to be limited; each courageous act will be viewed as justification for the recommendation of a corresponding medal so long as the act is worthy of acknowledgment and sets an example for the other members of the unit. All military personnel must clearly understand that participation in a dangerous mission cannot be looked upon automatically as justification for a recommendation of a medal award. Only in cases where difficulties and obstacles are encountered can command ranks have the opportunity to witness the courageous acts of their subordinates. And only under these circumstances can erroneous evaluation and inadequate recommendations be prevented.

f) Through reports from Corps Tactical Zones and Division Tactical Areas, the Joint General Staff has discovered that foreign military personnel serving as advisors to Vietnam units have been appropriately cited, while personnel serving in allied units that are fighting in Vietnam are usually not cited by Vietnamese authorities. Although in staff, technical, training, or other areas they have notdirectly assisted the Republic of Vietnam Armed Forces in the same way as those personnel in Advisory teams, they can be recommended for a corresponding Vietnamese medal, even though, in from the standpoint of combat, they have not had the opportunity to achieve anything outstanding in the way of territorial pacification. Corps Tactical Zone and Division Tactical Area Commanders should be more aware of the merits of these people in order to grant an equitable and appropriate award regardless of the origin of these worthy soldiers.

g) In creating many types of new medals, addressees should distinguish the following:

-The Gallantry Cross is intended for courageous acts in combat against the enemy (for the Army, Navy and Air Force).

-The Air Gallantry Medal is intended for courageous acts, which includes professional skill exhibited in an aircraft in distress as a result of technical failure, poor weather condition or due to combat.

-The Navy Gallantry Medal is intended for courageous acts, which includes professional skill exhibited in a war vessel when that vessel is in distress while underway as a result of technical failure, poor weather conditions, or due to combat, or any other cause of distress.

-The Hazardous Service Medal is intended for courageous acts performed outside of combat.

-The Life Saving Medal is intended for courageous acts and self-sacrifice while entering a dangerous area to rescue other people in distress.

h) Usually, recommending officials and awarding authorities, due to excessive workloads, do not have sufficient time to thoroughly evaluate the conditions and procedures for awarding the different types of medals, particularly this is true regarding new medals, the total of which has increased considerably. Therefore, officers of the Adjutant General Division must act as advisors to unit commanders in all matters relating to this field. At the same time, unit commanders should give officers of the Adjutant General Division a share of the responsibility in this field before submitting recommendations.

i) Recommending officials must allow the awarding authority a minimal period for consideration and preparation of an award in order to obtain best results. This period is prescribed as one week from the date the awarding authority receives the recommendation.

V. The medals listing in this Memorandum are considered appropriate in this time of war. The Joint General Staff will make a study to prescribe the conditions and procedures for awarding a number of new medals in accordance with the prescribed plan and program. Agencies should not confuse this plan by requesting the immediate awarding of this medal or another type of medal. The difficulties in consideration the desire to obtain the best results requires must time in consultation in order to avoid duplications.

The Joint General Staff reminds agencies that they should not recommend new medals that are not yet prescribed in this Memorandum. These recommendations will not be considered.

This Memorandum is to be given the widest dissemination, at least to company level commanders, who are the lowest recommending officials in the command system.

APO 4002, 30 March 1966

Lieutenant General Cao Van Vien
Chief of Joint General Staff
Republic of Vietnam Armed Forces

QUÂN-PHỤC SĨ-QUAN LỤC-QUÂN

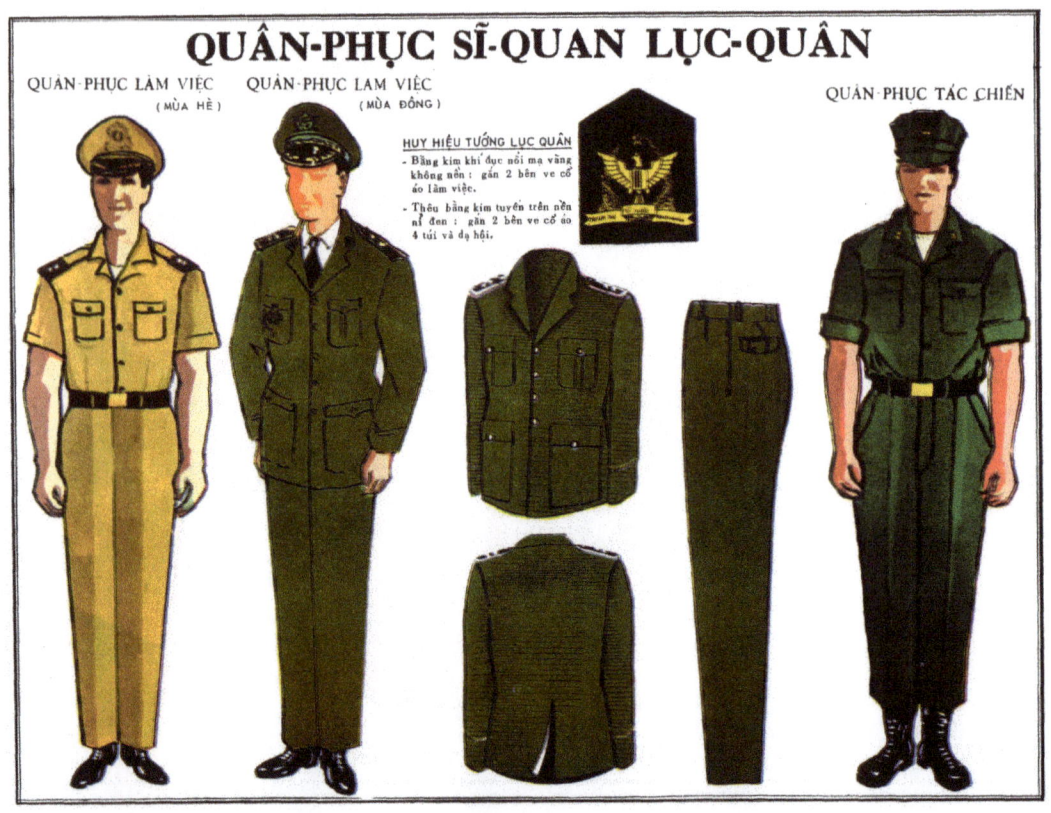

CẤP HIỆU SĨ-QUAN CẤP TÁ VÀ ÚY LỤC-QUÂN

ĐẠI LỄ và TIỂU LỄ CẦU VAI		LÀM VIỆC
	Đại Tá	
	Trung Tá	
	Thiếu Tá	
	Đại Úy	
	Trung Úy	
	Thiếu Úy	

HUY HIỆU MŨ LỤC QUÂN VÀ ĐỊA PHƯƠNG QUÂN

CẤP TƯỚNG — CẤP ÚY CẤP TÁ

CẤP HẠ SĨ QUAN VÀ BINH SĨ — Huy hiệu Mũ Địa Phương Quân và Nghĩa Quân

Army of the Republic of Vietnam Insignia

Group 1, Ministry of National Defense, Joint General Staff, I Corp, II Corps, III Corps, IV Corps, Capital Military Zone, 1st Division, 2d Division, 5th Division, 7th Division, 9th Division.
Group 2, 18TH Division 21st Division, 22nd Division, 23RD Division, 25th Division, Marines, Airborne Division, Special Forces Rangers, Military Police, Free World Forces, Military Bands
Group 3, Engineer Corps, 5th Engineer Group, Signal Corps, 61st Signal Group, Transportation, Political Warfare, Buddhist Chaplain, Catholic Chaplain, Protestant, Psychological Warfare, Political Training, Military Supply Corps. **Group 4**, Regional and Popular Forces, Artillery Headquarters, 34th Artillery Battalion, Armor Corps, 1st Armored Squadron, Finance and Administration, Military Justice, Welfare for the Children of Fallen Soldiers, 1st, 2d, 3rd And 4th Logistical Headquarters

Navy Insignia, Navy HQ, Fleet HQ, Navy Medical Center, Escort Ship Tuy-Dong, 22nd Sea Div., Hoa-Van 471 Oiler, LST Tam-Set (Battle Axe)331, LST Thi_Nai 502, LST Doan-Tang 228, Minesweeping Craft, Costal Patrol Craft (Golden Turtle), LLST "Sacred Arrow"

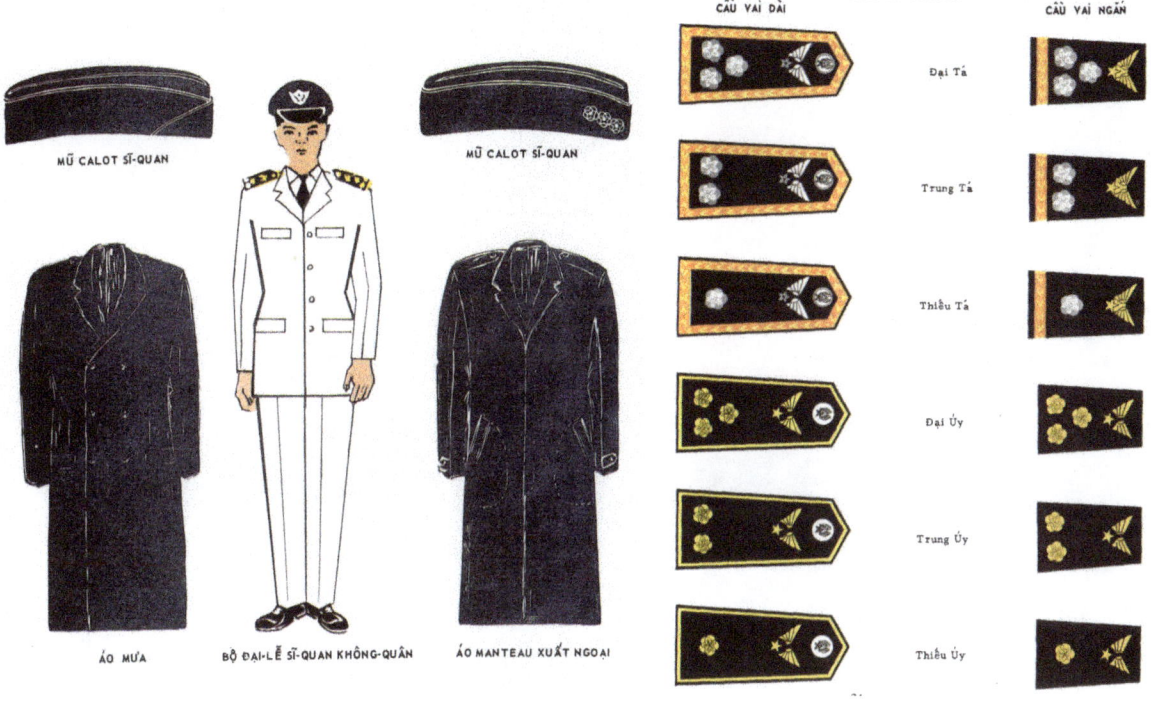

Air Force insignia: Air Force HQ, Air Force operations center, technical and supply wing, Air Force training center, medical evaluation center, 23rd, 33rd, 41st wings, 62nd, 74th wings, 413, 415 squadrons

Group 2 514, 516, 5/22, 211 Squadrons, 213, 215, 217, 110 Squadrons, 92nd Wing, 112, 114, 116 Squadrons.

Examples of RVNAF Shoulder Sleeve Insignia
From the 1970s

South Vietnamese Medals with Certificates

23. Armed Forces Honor Medal First Class
pg. 34-35

16. Gallantry Cross
pg. 31

73. Ethnic Development Medal First Class
pg. 64

63. Psychological Warfare Medal First Class and Second Class **pg. 61**

Starting at the top left-hand corner is a Vietnamese Army parachute badge, to the right is a Ranger insignia followed by a Lieut. Col. rank insignia. The second row shows a variation of the Army parachute insignia with a Special Forces basic parachute badge and a captains rank insignia. The third row has a RVN PRU Provincial Reconnaissance Unit metal Beret Badge, with a Special Forces senior parachutist badge and set of South Vietnamese pilot wings. The fourth row shows a Master Special Forces parachute badge and a Republic of Vietnam Air Force insignia. On the bottom row the hand holding a sword with a wing is the active airborne insignia for those on jump status and to the right is a French made airborne insignia as well as 2 cloth Army parachute wings, the top being a basic parachute badge and the bottom being a Vietnamese army master parachute badge. The small round badge is a Vietnamese Army Second Corps.

99

This display starting in the upper left-hand corner is an original Gallantry Cross with palm. The cross itself is almost black and there is some discussion that it was awarded for soldiers killed in action. Adjacent to the Vietnamese Gallantry Cross with palm is an American-made version with the Palm being noticeably larger. To the right of these two medals are three American variations of the Vietnamese Wound Medal. It is not exactly clear why there are so many American-made versions of the Vietnamese medal since any American wounded would receive the Purple Heart Medal and not be eligible for Vietnamese award.

On the second row is a Vietnamese version of the Honor Medal second class with an American version to the right. The third medal is Vietnamese Army Meritorious Service Medal made in America and generally sold with the incorrect ribbon as shown here. The correct Vietnamese ribbon is brown, green, and red as shown in the color plates.

The next-to-last medal is The Cross for Military Valor (French: Croix de la Valeur Militaire) and is a military decoration of France. It recognizes an individual for showing valor in presence of an enemy, in theatres of operations which are not subject to the award of the Croix de guerre des théâtres d'opérations extérieures (Cross of War for Foreign Theatres of Operations). The Cross for Military Valor is usually awarded for security or peacekeeping operations, always outside the French territory. It is shown to point out it would not have been awarded by the French to soldiers serving in Vietnam since the French never considered that a peace keeping mission. The final military medal is the French Indochina medal in gilt which is how the later versions were presented.

This display is of various miniature medal examples starting with 2 French miniatures of the Legion of Honor and the French Military Merit medal. The next miniature is Vietnamese and still mounted to the shop keeper's card from Saigon. The next 2 medals are a Vietnamese version of the Air Service Medal and an American version. The bottom 2 rows show American made versions of Vietnamese Miniature medals

American Commemorative Medals for the Vietnam War

After the fall of the Republic and years passed, commemorative medals for veterans begin to appear in honor of significant events during the fighting. Not surprisingly the first was a commemorative medal in honor of the Vietnamese Cross of Gallantry Unit Citation that came out along with one for the Civil Action Unit award.

A very unique commemorative medal honors those who fought during Tet and saw their victory turned to a defeat by the media. The U.S. made Commeoratives shown all seemed to be manufactured to same quality and specifications as official American military medals.

RVN Gallantry Cross Unit Citation Commemorative Medal

Qualifying Dates: 1965-1973

Criteria: Struck to honor all soldiers, sailors, marines, airmen and Allies who were awarded the RVN Gallantry Cross Unit Citation.

RVN Civil Action Unit Citation Commemorative Medal

Qualifying Dates: 1965-1973

Criteria: Struck to honor all soldiers, sailors, marines, airmen and Allies who were awarded the RVN Civil Action Honor Unit Citation.

Combat Action Commemorative Medal

Qualifying Dates: 1941-TBD

Criteria: Struck to honor all Soldiers and Airmen who served in Comat.

Combat Action Commemorative Medal

Qualifying Dates: 1941-TBD

Criteria: Struck to honor all, Sailors and Marines who served in Comat.

Presidential Unit Citation Commemorative Medal

Qualifying Dates: 1941-TBD

Criteria: Struck to honor all members of the U.S. Armed Forces who recieved the Presidential Unit Citation.

Meritorious Unit Citation Commemorative Medal

Qualifying Dates: 1941-TBD

Criteria: Struck to honor all members of the U.S. Armed Forces who recieved the Meritorious Unit Citation.

TeT Offensive Commemorative Medal

Qualifying Dates: 1941-TBD

Criteria: Struck to honor all, U.S. and Allied Forces who served during the 1968 TeT Offensive.

Airborne & Air Assault Commemorative Medal

Qualifying Dates: 1941-TBD

Criteria: Struck to honor all Soldiers and Marines who made airborne or air assault operations.

BIBLIOGRAPHY

Joint General Staff, Ministry of Defense <u>Huy-Chương Ân-Thưởng trong Quân-Lực Viêtnam Công-Hòa (Medals given in the Republic of Vietnam Armed Forces).</u> Saïgon, 1969. (An authoritative official publication in Vietnamese and English on the military awards, well illustrated.)

Ministry of Interior, "Bảng-Kê Các Loại Huy-Chương Dân-Sự Việtnam" (Descriptive list of the Varieties of Vietnamese Civil Medals"), Saigon, undated. (A description without illustrations of the civil medals and conditions for award.)

Vietnam Council on Foreign Relations, <u>Awards and Decorations of Vietnam,</u> Saigon, 1972. (Colored illustrations and conditions for award of both military and civil medals, an unfortunately scarce book.)

Nghi-Đinh Số 1285-a/TTP/VP ngày 12-8-1057 ân-định các đẳng cấp cua huy-chương "Kim-Khánh" (Decree #1285-a/TTP/VP of August 12, 1957 determining the grades of the medal "Kim-Khánh"). (Extract of official regulations)

Joint General Staff, Ministry of Defense, <u>Huấn-Lênh Điều-Hành Căn-Bản về Cấp-Hiêu, Quân-Phuc Quân-Kỳ, Lệnh-Kỳ và Phù-Hiêu của QLVNCH,</u> Saigon, undated. (A color manual of ARVN uniforms, medals, flags, and insignia, recently reprinted in Hong Kong by Mr. Louis Cheng.)

Joint General Staff, Ministry of Defense Memorandum No. 910/TTM/VP/PCP/3 (translation), Saigon, March 30, 1966. (Instruction on the procedures for the recommendations for awards for fifteen of the military medals.)

Chancellory, Ministry of Defense, State of Vietnam, Letter No. 481/QP/CA. Saigon, June 12, 1954. (An official letter transmitting to the Military Attache of the American Embassy in Saigon orders and decrees concerning the national decorations.)

Attention is also called to the books by Mr. Bob Heller and Mr. Daniel Byrne and to the many fine articles by Mr. C. V. Kelly, Lt. F. C. Brown, Mr. V. R. Brook, Major Duan K. Sinclair, Mr. James W. Peterson, and others, particularly in <u>The Medal Collector</u>. Of special interest is the fine article by Mr. Kelly in <u>The Medal Collector</u> of October 1977 on the Vietnamese Star of the November Revolution, an apparent pattern for an abortive star to be awarded the principal officers who participated in the coup 'against Diem.

Particular attention is also called to the excellent color illustrated article by the late Col. Paul Rullier on some projected awards of the State of Vietnam, "Les Decorations de l' Etat du Vietnam de 1945 a 1955, <u>Symboles & Traditions</u>", No. 122, April-June 1987, pp. 41-51.

The Decorations and Medals of the Republic of Vietnam and Her Allies, 1950 through 1975. by John Sylvester and Col. Frank Foster

Press

Other Great Medals and Insignia Books All Available at WWW.MOAPress.com or on Amazon

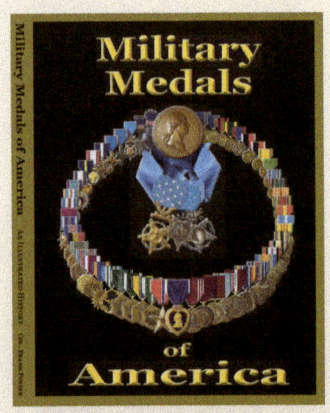

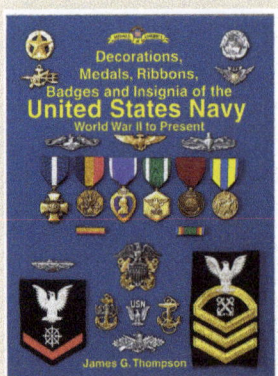
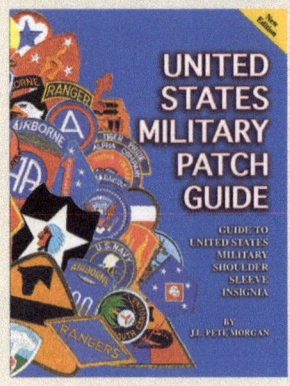

America's Best Medal and Ribbon Wear Guides All Available at WWW.MOAPress.com or on Amazon

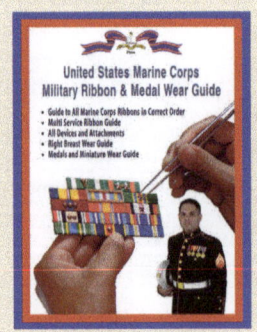
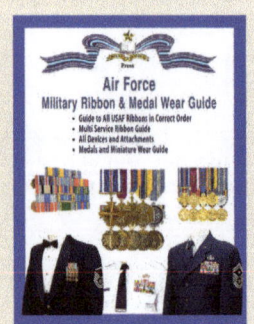

www.ingramcontent.com/pod-product-compliance
Lightning Source LLC
Chambersburg PA
CBHW042027100526
44587CB00029B/4320